Written Off:

How One Man's Journey Through Poverty, Disability and Delinquency Is Transforming The Juvenile Justice System

by

Hasan Davis, J.D.

Disclaimer: The contents of this book are my recollections of more than 40 years of memories and experiences. I recognize, as my mother has pointed out, that others may remember them differently. It is not my intention to hurt anyone in the telling of my story. I am proud of the fact that I have built, maintained, or repaired many of the connections that were damaged in my early life, finding and sometimes giving forgiveness in order to move forward in my life and relationships.

First edition 2016

ISBN: 978-0-9971558-0-8
Printed in the USA

Hasan Davis J.D.
Founder, HD Solutions
Project Director, College for Every Student
For information about booking Hasan for a conference keynote or workshop, to engage him as a consultant, or for media interviews, please contact him at:
859-200-0598
www.hasandavis.com
Hasan@hasandavis.com

Contributing Author: Yael Cohen, M.A, Special Education Advocate and Bestselling Author of *Secrets of a Special Education Advocate: Supercharge Your Child's Special Ed IEP So Your Child Can Excel*

Photo/Design Credits:

Cover designed by J. Bruce Jones http://www.brucejonesdesign.com

Alice Lovelace photo in Epilogue taken by Nic Paget-Clarke

Cover photo of Hasan Davis taken by Chris Radcliffe, http://www.chrisradcliffephotography.com (Photo Courtesy of Integrated Marketing & Communications at Berea College. First appeared in Volume 85 Number 3 of Berea College Magazine Winter 2014

Photo captions are on the last page of the book.

Find a typo? Please email us hasan@hasandavis.com so we can fix it in a future edition.

Chief Editors: Carly Carruthers, Alice Lovelace, Yael J. Cohen

Yael J. Cohen, Publisher

DEDICATION

This book is dedicated to all of the Hope Dealers who choose to explore what is possible instead of just lamenting over what is present.

The friends and loved ones whose support over the years has continued to ground me and push me forward into my work as a champion of children.

To my Fellows, who have helped my sharpen my skills and focus my commitment. There are too many to name, but your presence is what gives me the courage to tell my story.

To my mother, Alice Lovelace, who blessed all of her children with wings and inspired them to find a reason to fly. Thank you for the gift of your in wavering support and encouragement at every step of my journey. You told me that my victory was inevitable, and I believed . . . your faith made all of the difference in my world.

To my father Charles "Jikki" Riley, who passed too soon. Thank you for choosing me as your son and teaching me how to be a man. Your examples of perseverance and compassion were the light I followed out of my darkest days.

To Dr. Lorraine Wilson, who imagined a school in which individualized education could carry every child to the next horizon. Thank you for peering behind my mask.

To Patty and the Sims, who created safe space and a second family for any child who needed more of both. Thank you from me and all the lost boys you sheltered.

To Kentucky's Governor Steve Beshear and First Lady Jane Beshear, along with the Secretary Brown of the Kentucky Justice and Public Safety Cabinet: You were all instrumental in giving us the opportunity to transform a justice system into a real child-serving system.

And a special thank you to the love of my life, Dreama Gentry, who was brave enough to imagine that a angry and broken boy might one day become a strong partner and loving father. Thank you for picking up where the other great women left off. Without you, I think this life of mine would be a shadow of itself, and of little use to the world. You, Malcolm, and Christopher are the love that calms my fears and the presence that confirms my faith. Thank you for not giving up on the possibility of us.

TABLE OF CONTENTS

INTRODUCTION

DR. MAYA ANGELOU IMPACTS MY LIFE

"For those of us who chose this important work, hope is mandatory. Because, we cannot give what we do not possess." Hasan Davis J.D.

To this day, I do not understand how or why, out of the 1,500 hard-working students at Berea College, I was given the honor of welcoming Dr. Maya Angelou to campus. Thinking back on it, I may have appointed myself. It was the spring of 1988, just a few weeks into my first semester back after being expelled, and I was already struggling. I decided to put all my troubles aside and welcome Dr. Angelou and Alex Haley, the author of Roots, in the Green Room at Phelps Stokes Chapel prior to their speaking at one of our amazing convocations. At the time, Alex Haley was a member of the Berea College Board of Directors and a fierce supporter of Berea's mission. Maya Angelou was an audacious and fierce champion of hope. Without fear, she spoke light into dark places.

My self-appointed job was to keep them company while we waited for the Convocation to begin. With a smile on my face, I skipped afternoon classes to arrive early, as I was afraid I might get caught up in distractions and forget. I was nervous, so I coached myself through the best way to explain who I was to two living legends. About twenty minutes into my rehearsal, the door creaked open and, without fanfare or entourage and only a student escort, in they walked. I rushed to the door, extended my hand, and Maya Angelou caught me as I stumbled. She firmly grasped my hand; I immediately calmed.

I stood silent; she gave me a considered look, and then whispered in my ear, *"I am sure you have quite a story to share with the world, young man."* I froze, all fear. How could she learn of my challenges here at Berea in such a short time on campus? For two seconds, I relived the feeling of being an imposter while thoughts of my past failures seized me. "Do not *worry,*" she continued while holding my one hand firmly in both of her hands. *"You just have to finish writing the ending."* That said, her smile broadened and my calm was restored.

She introduced me to Alex Haley then directed me to sit with them and tell them about my student life. *"Me?"* I thought, *"They really want to know about me?* I sat and they stared. I felt exalted and blessed while they waited patiently for me to begin. Actually, I can't remember even one story I told them. I placed myself in God's hands and accepted that what they requested was offered in sincerity—a real desire by these two universally celebrated people to know how I fought my way back to become a second-time freshman at Berea College. A knock on the door announced it was time to start. Standing, I shook hands with Mr. Haley, thanked him for his time and his work, and then turned as Maya Angelou stood, raising my head to follow the rise of her calm face. Again, she took me by the hand and whispered, *"I am waiting for you to finish your story."* She smiled, handed me a piece of paper from her notebook, and walked out the door toward the stage and the packed auditorium. On the paper was her contact information. I still have that piece of paper. Her whispered wish for me became a part of all that drives me to continue writing my story.

Even though my story is not yet complete, I decided it was finally time to take Maya Angelou's advice and share some of the journey that took me from Hasan Davis, Juvenile Delinquent to Hasan Davis, Jurist Doctor. This is not just a memoir or autobiography, but a story of a child who was written off until Hope Dealers reclaimed and rebuilt him. They helped him find purpose and believe in his own intelligence and worth.

As a juvenile justice professional, I have spent twenty years watching child-serving systems fail at the singular task of rebuilding and rescuing children. Rehabilitative systems had been reduced to punitive systems and support and services for children and families in crisis eliminated. I finally realized there existed an opportunity to create a different conversation, a conversation about how we serve young people and how we create the possibility of success in spite of their challenges. Very often, I see myself reflected in the stories of so many young people, and I realize the only reason I was able to transform my life was a committed group of adult champions who refused to let me fail.

All children deserve someone who can see them as they imagine themselves instead of just as they are in the present moment. All children deserve a Hope Dealer who is willing to believe beyond logic and help them reach their greatest potential in work, education, and as contributors to their communities.

When you reach the end of this story, which is not the end of my story, I hope you are inspired to stand with me in opposition to the incarceration of children in juvenile prisons. I hope you will join me in supporting the building of better networks of services for youth and families--networks that allow them to move past their poverty, disabilities, race, trauma, and delinquency to become productive, engaged contributors to society.

Someone is waiting for you to be his or her "Hope Dealer," an audacious and fearless champion for children.

CHAPTER ONE

A CHALLENGING CHILDHOOD

*"At an early age, it seemed clear that life for me would be an endless series
of challenges to my very existence, or it would be nothing at all."*
Hasan Davis, J.D.

Things Fall Apart

Despite my mother's care and best intentions, I entered the school to prison pipeline in St. Louis, Missouri at the age of seven years. I was in the 1st grade. For me, the trauma began when my teacher locked me in the coatroom for several days, probably because I could not sit quietly at my desk.

I now know that I had ADHD and dyslexia. However, back in 1973, neither condition was a typical diagnosis for schoolchildren. Kids who couldn't sit still and do their school work were considered behavior problems. Children with dyslexia were often referred to as a "retarded readers" or called "dumb" or "lazy." I couldn't copy or write what the teacher asked us to and my handwriting was illegible even though I spoke well. I could not follow rapid or complicated instructions, and I had impulse control issues. It would be three more years before the country even had a law about special education; many children with disabilities did not attend school and simply stayed home. It would be many more years until teachers were trained on how to handle kids like me.

I also had secrets in my personal life that compounded my already challenged existence. In addition to my undiagnosed disabilities, my mother left my father, Fred, to return to her family in St. Louis when I was three because of a long history of domestic violence. We moved around, staying with various family members because Mom could not afford the combination of day care, food, and rent. She tried to create a stable environment for us while working two jobs, and Mom was so happy when she was able to buy a house and move us to Farlin Avenue in North St. Louis.

Within months, Fred followed her to St. Louis. For many years, my parents tried to make the marriage work, even giving birth to Shawnta and Tony in the process. Unfortunately, after a while, the pattern of abuse re-emerged. The same year I entered first grade, my sister and I witnessed a life-threatening attack on our mom. I've always believed the only reason he did not kill her was because my sister, Theresa, and I ran to the kitchen, grabbed knives, and threatened him. We then called the police and watched as any remaining childhood fantasy of growing up in a house

6

protected by a loving father dissipated. A full separation followed and then divorce. Things fell apart.

It would be another thirty years before research on the effects of trauma on child and adolescent development would lead to trauma-informed care models of teaching. These models help educators better understand the complex needs of individual children, and provide teachers the tools to meet these children where they are and lead them to success, in spite of their early difficulties.

Back then, I was simply a poor, black boy with attention and behavior problems who could not understand simple lessons and could not grasp the basic building blocks of education. In my teachers' eyes, I was easy to label as "retarded," as they referred to children with intellectual disabilities, despite what I know now, that I am an "engaged learner." Experiences in my life and my exposure to the world of art have taught me that when I am in a room of high-functioning people, I step up to the edge with them; I engage and function at a high level. However, if you put me in a room of low-functioning, unengaged learners, or simply lock me in a coatroom, I tend to sink to the lowest denominator.

Hope Dealer #1

Ever since I can remember, my mother advocated attacking our problems head on. She always asked three questions: How did you get into this situation? What have you learned from your situation? What do you want to happen? She helped us develop our minds and asked us to think through problems. She taught us that making a decision is an act of power and that not making a decision is an act of submission to someone else's expectations.

When we moved and Mom first enrolled us in Ashland Elementary School, I was very excited to start first grade because it was a new school. Preschool and both of my kindergarten classes had not been ideal; school was tough for me. As I would think many times growing up, I hoped that moving and going to a new school might come with a brand new opportunity. I needed a new opportunity because, at the time, I was already "that kid" - the one who was always in trouble.

Shortly into my first grade year, I began to feel all alone in my struggles as the other kids were learning to read much faster than I was, and they were all so much better at sitting still. There was nowhere at school to turn for help, and I had no words to explain what was going on in my head.

Unfortunately, my first grade teacher chose to throw me away. I was put into the coatroom, terrified, embarrassed, and angry. As an adult looking back, I can only remember disregard and disdain for me, and can still feel that awful pain.

As I sat in the coatroom, I immediately shut down. I never told my mother what was happening during my first days of school. I told her everything was okay, and the teacher never contacted my mother.

After spending a day or so in the coatroom, I stopped beating myself up for being so stupid and embarrassing my family. I was emotionally spent, filled with dread at all the different ways I feared my mother and others would respond to my situation. I stopped punching and kicking the mound of coats. I stopped crying. Resigned to my fate, I took a look around my *new classroom* and realized there was more to the

coatroom than just coats. There were lunches in paper bags and TV character lunchboxes. I thought about my mother's lessons and decided this could be a pretty positive outcome for a sorry situation.

Soon, I knew which kid had peanut butter and jelly sandwiches without the crust, who always brought fruit cups, and where to find the Tang Instant Breakfast Drink. I thought maybe my teacher actually did put me in the right place.

I stuffed myself. I was living with purpose! For a few days, I ate very well until the other mothers began asking why their kids were complaining that parts of their lunches were missing. An investigation into the mystery of the food theft was launched and it led them right to *my classroom*, the coatroom, where I happily sat with lunchboxes spread around me.

8

My mother never went ballistic when she encountered the public school system. Instead, she became calm and clear about what she expected. It was always clear when she finished talking to my teacher that when it came to her son, she didn't care what they *usually* did.

When I was steered towards a special education class or when I was secretly removed to a closet, my mother, from my very first week of school, bypassed the office and showed up in my classroom. Her message was always straightforward. *"You will not isolate my child for any reason. You will not banish my child to the hallway to do his work. You will let me know if you have a problem, any problem, with my child."*

My mother was, and still is, my fiercest advocate; she promised me that we would figure out a path to success together. By the time she left the school that day, I had been returned to the Classroom Learning Zone. To save face, my teacher put me back with my classmates while assuring everyone she would keep her eyes on me.

When I got older and asked, my mother told me she showed up at Ashland Elementary School that day prepared to confront my teacher because I was being overly evasive when she questioned me about what I was learning. She continued to show up unannounced, sometimes just to stand outside our classroom doors and listen, even when our growing family was spread between three middles and two high schools.

As you will note, this level of intervention from an adult ally occurred over and over during my child and young adulthood. I was so very lucky to have had caring adults advocating for me; many children did not and do not. I succeeded against the odds to find "a way from no way." I am grateful for my Hope Dealers and the core strength I inherited from my mother.

Nothing To Lose

Our new home also brought with it another failed new opportunity—a family of bullies who lived down the street and took an instant dislike to my siblings and me. Not only did I have to deal with their bullying at home while playing outside, but it seeped into my school life as well. Lisa, the youngest girl in the family, was in my grade and even in my class some years.

Second grade went by in kind of a blur, with more academic and social struggles. By the time third grade came around, I knew I had to do something different in order to fit in or I was going to be the patsy for every bully. I discovered I had an exceptional talent for risk-taking. In hindsight, I did things that were not very smart. For example, after being dared by some of my friends, I climbed up on the wall that separated the lower elementary and upper elementary and waited for the older boys to notice me. I recognized a couple of big boys who bullied me, including Lisa's oldest brother, as they came into the schoolyard, strutting their stuff and acting like they were in charge. I jumped off the top of the wall between the two schoolyards and ploughed into them. They fell on their butts on the asphalt, and sat stunned for a moment. My classmates looked at me with awe and surprise as I jumped up and began to run for my life.

They chased me from the upper grade yard towards the elementary yard, where I was hoping a teacher would see and intervene before they reached me. Unfortunately, maybe for the first time in my elementary career, there were no teachers around to see me running fast and recklessly. I made it all the way back to the ten-foot fence that surrounded our end of the schoolyard, and then realized that the only way out was up and over the fence. I was three quarters of the way up when I realized no one was following me.

Thinking my escape was guaranteed, I happily started to scale the top of the fence when a big sixth grader charged it like a cannonball, hitting it so hard that the fence wobbled twenty feet in every direction. I fell back onto the concrete schoolyard and they descended on me, with all fists and feet like an old Kung Fu movie.

Just then, Miss Moore, my third grade teacher, blew her whistle, screamed, and everybody froze. She pulled me from under the pile of boys. Although I was frequently dragged in to her classroom to make the acquaintance of her duct tape covered fishing rod, for the first time that year, I actually felt safer being dragged in. Third grade was looking up. My classmates began calling me fearless and crazy, which increased after I

10

volunteered to be the Indian when playing Cowboys and Indians. (They didn't know I was working on a different ending to the saga.)

I Know Who I Am

After the upper yard incident, my social life at school improved some, but I still faced challenges. The next thing that fired my anger was when I received my first social studies book. Miss Moore went on and on about the important people we would read about in this book – the people who made America great. I tore through the book, page after page, looking for the chapter that confirmed my great place in this nation's story. Chapter after chapter, I found nothing. Finally, at the back of the book, I found a picture of a black man with a scarred back. The caption beneath the picture simply read, *"The American Negro Slave."*

I was so angry because I knew better. My mother had spent lots of time teaching us about ancient African kingdoms from Timbuktu to Nubia and about brave American heroes like Harriet Tubman and Frederick Douglas. I even knew about Crispus Attucks and the American Revolution. Sadly, in third grade, I began my struggle with the story of slavery that is glossed over in this country, a story that did not include the courage and perseverance that I had been taught at home was part of my people's identity.

The Writing on the Wall

I think my behavior in third grade scared my mother, and taking the family out to dinner, she announced a bold decision. She said we were moving to Atlanta, Georgia. My two sisters, Theresa and Shawnta, and my youngest brother, Tony, were silent. (I believe one reason for her bravery was her new relationship with Charles Riley, Jr., son of St. Louis's own Featherweight Boxing Champ "Chillin' Charlie Riley." We called him by his nickname, Jikki, and all loved him.)

In April 1976, my siblings and I were sent to live with one of my mother's six sisters. The house was put up for sale; mom quit her job, and, with my soon-to-be stepfather, made her way to Atlanta to prepare for us. Mom and Jikki knew no one in Atlanta, but a friend of my grandmother on my father's side offered to give them a room until they got settled.

At the end of the school year, my mom sent for us. My grandmother, Theresa Davis, who my oldest sister is named after, took us on an eighteen hour Greyhound bus ride. Once we left St. Louis, there were only a few places where it was safe for us to get off the bus. The great thing about having an old Southern grandma was she prepared for everything. She had a basket full of food that could feed a kingdom. It was a long ride south through Illinois, Indiana, Kentucky, and Tennessee.

The first apartment we had in Atlanta was on Ponce De Leon. It was an efficiency apartment with a fold out bed couch, a kitchenette, a toilet, and a stand up shower. The six of us lived there without much comfort, but we had each other. There was another kid who lived in our building and his mother was a prostitute, so he wound up spending a lot of time with us when she was working. We spent the summer going to the movies and taking long walks.

Before school started, we moved to Valley Estate Apartments in an area close to Fort McPherson. It was an apartment complex with lots of green and lots of land. One of the most interesting things that I experienced while in Valley Estate Apartments was returning from school one day to find all of the possessions of one of the families stacked at the street curb. They had a problem making the rent payment and had been evicted. There were strangers rummaging through their property. We spent the rest of the afternoon camped out with what was left of their furniture and personal effects until their parents brought cars and trucks to retrieve it.

I attended Central Park Elementary School for my fourth grade year. I remember learning to play the flute; the music came so easy compared to my other classes. One day, a kid informed me that, "All flute players are sissies." My efforts to prove him wrong by beating him with my flute led to my removal from the orchestra. I continued to be very frustrated by school because there was no acknowledgment of my need for assistance and no plan to provide me with support. I lived for the unstructured time, like recess, when I could talk to friends and run. It was during this time that I was able to escape the constant worry in the classroom over whether or not the teacher was going to call on me and ask me to read over and over until all of my classmates were staring and whispering about me as I tried to disappear. We lived in Valley Estates until the winter of my fifth grade school year when we suddenly moved.

Helping Hands

That winter was my first experience with the Hosea Williams Charity. Hosea Williams was a member of the Southern Christian Leadership Conference, which Dr. Martin Luther King had founded. Williams was very civic-minded and volunteer-focused, and a very popular member of the Atlanta, Georgia community. He tried to take care of as many people as he could. On major holidays, and especially on Christmas and Thanksgiving, the charity would put on a grand feast in downtown Atlanta at the Civic Center; they invited anyone in need to come to these events.

We went down to the Christmas event, and there was a huge hall in the Civic Center full of long tables with lots of volunteers and food everywhere. They gave each of us a Styrofoam compartmental plate, and we went down the food line. We received as much food as we could eat; there was turkey, dressing, mashed potatoes, macaroni and cheese, dessert, and sweet tea.

When we finally had as much food as we could eat, we each took a turn walking up onto the stage and sitting on Santa's lap. A volunteer took and then handed us a Polaroid photo which magically developed in front of our eyes. Then, an adult handed us a wrapped box, with the handwritten words *Boy 9 - 11* or *Girl 5 – 9*, matching us to our age-appropriate gift. That was all we got for Christmas that year.

We were a family of six and struggling. My mother was a tight budgeter, and sometimes all she could buy was what we absolutely needed. At Christmas time, the first thing to go, if money was tight, was buying a tree. That didn't mean we wouldn't have a tree; we would take the Christmas lights and pin them on the wall in the shape of a Christmas tree. Then we'd string popcorn and hard candy for our Christmas ornaments. At the base of the wall, under our homemade tree, is where we would place our gifts from the charity in addition to many more handmade gifts.

One of the things that I remember most about my childhood is that no matter how tight money was, no matter how often my mother juggled our finances to their limits and we had to move or ask for assistance, we always had each other.

New School, New Drama

After Christmas, we moved back to the city of Atlanta into an old house on Hardee Street, and my mother enrolled me in the second of my fifth grade classes. On my first day of school, I met a girl, Robyn, who was clearly high up in the pecking order of elementary school. She was "the pretty girl," the girl that everyone wanted to know or be.

For some reason, Robyn decided that the awkward, quiet, new kid, who was sitting at a table because there were no desks left in the room, would be fun to mess with. She asked me if I wanted to be her new boyfriend. Of course, being the new kid, having no friends, and having the most beautiful girl in the world asking you a simple question, there was only one answer. So, she told me I was her boyfriend and that I would need to do all the things that a boyfriend does: pick up her stuff, get her things, and make her happy.

However, I was out on the playground with my girlfriend during the first recess, when this huge monster of a kid yelled and rushed at me. With a crowd of kids gathering, he pushed me and asked me what I was doing with HIS girlfriend. I looked to Robyn for some kind of clarification. She just laughed, and after a couple of hard shoves from this giant kid, I decided that I'd had enough. Jikki always taught me you don't start fights if you can help it, but you also don't let people treat you a certain way for too long or they might try to make it a new habit. I remembered what it was like at Ashland when people thought they could treat me any way they wanted, and I decided then that it would never happen again. I introduced his face to the jungle gym, and Robyn began to scream hysterically, running over asking what I was doing to her boyfriend and why was I beating him up. I figured out pretty quickly that I was her mark, being used to make this goon jealous. I left the two of them on that playground beneath the jungle gym crying in each other's arms. That was the day I realized that I might not really understand girls.

Fortunately for me, I was only at this unmemorable school for about a month. On a cold night, Jikki woke all of us up and told us not to turn on the lights, but to grab what we had because it was time to go. There was a truck that he had already put our furniture inside of; we were moving again. We moved to Lyndon Club Apartments out in College Park. The next day, I started at Kathleen Mitchell Elementary. Despite my challenges with schoolwork, I didn't receive much support in class. In fact, the teachers ignored me for the most part, allowed me to sit and, in their words, "just do the best I could."

CHAPTER TWO

HEADED DOWN THE WRONG PATH

"Too often children wind up on the wrong side of the law by default, no one ever thinking to tell them that they actually have a choice in the matter."
Hasan Davis, J.D.

The Blessing of Family

During our time at Lyndon Club Apartments, we encountered our first clear, vivid experience with racism from a man named Winston; he and his family managed the apartments. Winston's cousin, Gill, was a member of the police department. Anytime there was an event at the clubhouse or in the apartments for residents, Gill would ensure only certain members of the apartment community were invited or given entry. This was a source of contention for us on a number of occasions. Even as kids, we were frustrated to be told that we didn't have a right to something because of the color of our skin.

In spite of dealing with Winston, Gill, and the adults in that community, there were a lot of opportunities for us. After school, Jikki  would help us with our homework then take us out to the woods and give us what he called "young ranger training." He taught us survival techniques, like how to start a fire from scratch, and self-defense techniques. Mom would get tickets to plays. We would go ice-skating at the luxury hotel, to the High Museum of Art, and take excursions to "Underground Atlanta." Sometimes we'd take the bus into downtown Atlanta, ride up on the glass elevator in the Peachtree Plaza Hotel to the top floor, and have lunch in the revolving restaurant overlooking the city. Next, we might go see an art exhibit or theatre performance, sometimes ending the evening with a Kung-Fu movie at the Rialto Theater. Whenever we had a working car, we would go on exciting trips to Lake Lanier or Sweetwater Creek. Back then, a trip to Stone Mountain was like traveling to another city.

Mom and Jikki were now married and Jikki had already become more of a father than our stepfather; we were family. My parents were artists and activists, who were engaged social justice champions. Thanks to them, we always found a way to entertain ourselves. We put on fantastic talent shows, so incredible that the neighbors all came and our friends wanted to be involved. The shows became grand spectacles put together with our own talent. I never had  the sense that I did not have all that I needed because my parents ensured that we did not look, act, or behave as if we were poor. We were one family of millions, the working poor. I grew to believe that we were rich, maybe not in the influence of our pockets, but in the richness and influence of our experiences.

For fun, we'd get out our homemade bicycles, which we'd cobbled together from parts and pieces we had managed to acquire, and ride up to Old National Highway, to the grocery and Service Merchandise stores. As we got more frustrated with the way we were treated as black boys living in unincorporated Fulton County, with no social organizations, parks or recreation, or access to opportunity, either by conspicuous absence or malicious exclusion, we were able to justify our behavior more easily. We'd go inside the stores and shoplift, taking what we couldn't buy. Then we would return to the apartment complex and have our own parties. Sometimes we'd break into vacant apartments and invite all the other kids over; we embraced being rebellious and wild.

Delinquent

College Park, where the Lyndon Club Apartments were located, was less than ten miles from Atlanta, but a world away when it came to racial tolerance and quality education for blacks. We were routinely spat at when out walking, or people would throw whatever they were drinking out the car window onto us. I was once chased more than a mile through the woods and across the train tracks by a group of men driving a truck with a horn that sounded like the car from *The Dukes of Hazard*. We lived in Lyndon Club Apartments through the end of my fifth grade school year at Kathleen Mitchell Elementary School.

Shortly before we moved from Lyndon Club Apartments, Sean, Jikki's son from a previous relationship, came to live with us. He was nine, two years younger than I was. He was suffering from trauma, the result of multiple adverse childhood experiences. His birth mother and her acquaintances had abused him. He had scars all over his body and cigarette burns up and down his arms. Like us, he had seen many difficult times. Unlike us, he did not have a force like my own mother in his life to help him through when those dark times occurred. Sean always thought of himself as the black sheep of the family, and he often resorted to self-imposed isolation from us. He was confrontational, defensive, and aggressive, full of self-doubt, and mistrustful of all institutions and system. He believed it was impossible that anyone could love him for who he was. This thinking shaped how he saw the rest of the world.

After fifth grade, we moved a few miles away to Salem South Apartments where my old friend Rodney lived. I was enrolled into Brookview Elementary School in the sixth grade where I hung out with Rodney and a few new friends: Gerald, Daryl, and Dwayne. Every once in a while, Steve, Rodney's cousin, came over from Lyndon Club to visit. Steve was the oldest of my group of friends, and the most reckless. He had a long scar under his left eye from a fight he had when he was younger, and he carried a knife. He was very brash, angry, and unapologetic. Steve and the other boys became the core of my social group. We played tackle football on the gravel, went off into the woods, made forts, and rode our bikes all the way up to the highway; we were young people exploring what little of the world we could.

One Sunday morning, we all decided we should go up to the mall and hang out around Old National Highway near the Service Merchandise store and the supermarket. I asked my mother if I could go up with my friends. Knowing us the way she did, she gave me money for a Sunday paper and told me that I needed to return with her Sunday paper or there would be consequences. We all made our way up the couple of miles it took to cross the train tracks and go out to Old National Highway. We went into Service Merchandise and spent some time walking around. Gerald, my best friend, had a fixation with Legos. We stood in the Lego department where he complained about the fact that he didn't get Legos for Christmas and how his little sister wanted Legos too. Concerned, I told him this was not the time to be messing with these people's stuff.

I saw two plain-clothes security guards circling us in the store, and I knew there had to be more. I left Gerald with that warning and went to see if I could find the paper. Suddenly, I heard screaming coming from the toy department. I looked back to see a store employee holding Gerald by the collar of his shirt and walking toward me.

I also saw Daryl, Dwayne, and Steve coming from the other direction, and several other employees circling. I realized they were all coming after us. I gave a warning, and we exited the store as quickly as we could; the four of us left Gerald to his own devices.

We wandered around the stores a little longer, then went to the grocery store and found something to eat. As we left, I realized I had forgotten to get my mother's paper, but luckily, there was a paper machine box right outside of the store entrance. As I started putting the money in, I heard another shout. I looked up, and the same employee who had held Gerald in the Service Merchandise was walking toward us with Gerald beside him. He was screaming and pointing toward the parking lot. I looked to the parking lot and saw a police car turning into the parking lot. We scattered.

A few doors from the grocery store was a laundromat we used a number of times, so we knew there was a backdoor that led to the back of the store. From there, we ran to the train tracks and through a cement quarry. We decided it would be best if we split up. Steve and Rodney continued along the train tracks, while Daryl and Dwayne took off in the opposite direction. I took off alone headed for Roosevelt Highway.

I was probably the first to get home. As soon as I told my mother I didn't have the newspaper, she told me I was going to get her a paper before the day was out. I told her they didn't have any more papers, which was a funny lie for me to choose to tell, and she told me to get my bike out because I would have to ride to another store a couple of miles away to get a paper. I told her the machine ate the money, so she reluctantly gave me more quarters. I jumped on my homemade bike and began my journey.

It was about a thirty-minute ride to the store, but I got the newspaper. I went back on Roosevelt Highway, which was always pretty scary because there was no bicycle lane and a lot of traffic. In fact, there were a number of times when we had been run off the road by folks cursing at us and calling out racial epitaphs, so we were very leery of riding our bikes on this road. As I was riding, I got the sense there was a car following me because the stream of cars passing me had stopped. I took this as a very bad sign, realized I might be in danger, and looked for the next side road, a dirt bike path we knew of that left the road and went across the train tracks. Just then, the car pulled up closer to me.

I could see it was a big white car, and as it pulled past, I saw "Police" written on it. I took a slight breath of relief until I glanced in the back window and realized that Daryl, Dwayne, Steve, Gerald, and Rodney were all in the car. The police officer quickly blocked me, ran me off the road, and then immediately jumped out of the car with his hand on his gun. He told me I should get into the car right away. I asked him what was going on, and he told me I didn't have the right to ask him any questions, but I needed to get into the car. I told him I couldn't leave my bike in the middle of nowhere; somebody would steal it. He finally agreed to let me ride the bike back to the apartment, but warned me if I tried anything, he was going to "run my little black ass over with his big white car." He asked if I understood what he was saying; I did.

I rode my bike back with him as my escort, and every time we came to one of those paths into the woods, he guided his car a little closer just to let me know he was watching. When we got a few blocks from the turn off and the underpass near our apartment, I ditched into the woods, cut across, and headed for home. When I got to my apartment and walked through the front door, I couldn't find my mother, so I went to Gerald's apartment in the next building.

I walked through the front door, and heard my mother in the living room on their phone because we didn't have a phone at the time. From the few seconds of conversation I heard, I realized she was talking to a lawyer. About that time, the police officer caught up with me and dragged me out to the car with Daryl, Dwayne, Steve, Rodney, and Gerald. We sat there for a while figuring out how we got there, and after a heated conversation and some stupid words, we were finally taken to the police station.

Once we arrived at the East Point Police Department, we saw Gill, who said he hadn't realized the call was for us. If he had, he would have taken it, and he was pretty sure all of us would not have made it to the police station. With that, of course, Steve jumped to his feet; there was screaming and a lot of stupid words being thrown back and forth. By the end of the day, we'd finally been processed, fingerprinted, and questioned, and our moms had started showing up.

For the first time, I realized we were living in a community with almost nothing but mothers. My stepfather, Jikki, was a pillar in the community, but he was the only male role model for all of these young boys. There were no other men, only women trying to raise boys. When the other moms showed up, they were beside themselves.

Now, as a professional in this work, what I know now is the moms were probably embarrassed and afraid. They were concerned for their boys because once the system gets a hold of a child, it doesn't let go without a fight. The moms arrived drenched in the kind of fear and frustration that comes out all rage and anger. Every one of my friends' mothers screamed their charges at the police and their sons.

"I had to take three busses to get here. I had to leave work early; this might make me lose my job. I'm shipping your butt off to your daddy; you got one more time. I got three other kids who don't do this shit; maybe I should let them lock you up!" I listened to the litany of complaints; it was what I expected.

As a professional in this work, I also now know that, whether it is in education, child welfare, or juvenile justice, there are parents who are struggling to keep things together. Any small ripple of life, any small bump, creates huge waves in their lives and in their process and progress. This is especially true for parents who are advocating for children dealing with challenges because the system often makes them fight for everything they get.

Still now, I see parents who come to their kids' schools and are righteously indignant. There's fear, there's embarrassment, there's concern because they want their children to have the best, but it all comes out as this montage of anger. In response, the schools put up walls and say, "Oh, they're just another 'fill in the blank' (black woman, poor person, welfare mom, etc.).

After witnessing the rage heaped on the heads of my friends, I grew afraid and nervous. I was still waiting for my mother's arrival. I figured after all I had put her through, she would surely be in lockstep with all the other mothers. I worked on my speech, feeding on my righteous indignation and rage.

Psyching myself up for our confrontation, I decided I would justify my stupid choices by making it somebody else's problem, and blaming it on being a black male living in a crazy world. I was going to have to show her my tough face and tell her to back up off me. I had never talked back to my mother like this in my life. I figured that this finally might be the time I had to "talk stupid" in order to save my life.

Waiting for my mother to borrow a vehicle and to get to the police station was an ordeal in and of itself. I began to fill up with anger and frustration as I thought about racism, poverty, and our home insecurity. I thought about my father, who had remarried and seemed to have the perfect life. His son, my stepbrother, also had what seemed like a perfect life with his own room, with his own bed, and his own TV, while I was sharing the bed with my two brothers. I considered all the negative, stressful things going on in my life that had led me down the road that eventually led to this moment.

When Mom arrived, she was very calm and put together, not excited or angry at all. She came in very quietly and did the paperwork. I sat and watched, realizing the longer she remained quiet and calm, the greater the chances were I was in big trouble. After she did the paperwork, she thanked the officers. I realized she might be thinking that if someone goes off like those other women had in the police station, there might be a chance she could get arrested; perhaps that was the reason she wasn't losing her mind. I figured once she got outside the police station, she would go off. I did what we call the "Near-Far-Near" walk, walking close enough to let everybody know that I was with her, but not close enough for her to reach me if she finally decided to explode. Still she said nothing.

Once she got to the car, I was afraid that once we got in route, she would jump on me, or something. I was extremely nervous, waiting for her to explode so that I could explode back. That way, I could justify myself and wouldn't have to own the fact that I made the choice to be this other person. I figured it was about saving face, and that was why she wasn't doing all that stereotypical stuff like the other mothers. My imagination was taking over completely. I sat in the car with no seat belt on, my hand on the doorknob, thinking I might have to bail out to get away from the impending rage.

I was waiting to justify myself and waiting for all of the rage that would have been very atypical of my mother. Given my actions, it was the only response I could imagine. What had started as a trip to the grocery store at 7:00 am on a Sunday was ending more than twelve hours later on a long, quiet, dark drive home. As we passed each streetlight, I snuck glances at her face, anticipating her breaking her silence. I finally found the courage to look directly at her, and when I did, I saw that she was crying deep, silent tears. When she finally looked down at me, she said, *"Baby, if you could see what I see every time that I look at you, you would know how great you are."*

Well, I had no idea what to do with that. Here I was, this broken boy who couldn't read, couldn't sit still, couldn't stay in the class, and now couldn't stay out of trouble. What she said to me was the last thing I expected to hear. I didn't know what to do with her words. It left me feeling confused and feeling dumb. After the hours she had no doubt spent with worry and embarrassment, and having to spend money she had to take from something else, how could that be all she had to say to me? I thought about this for the rest of the trip home, staying close to the door, just in case.

When we pulled up to the apartment, my brothers and sisters greeted me with hysterics. Jikki walked into the room, and in his quiet way, told me to meet him upstairs. He suggested that if I was prepared to act like a man, then maybe it was time I started being treated like a man. After he whipped me, he talked with me for a long time about the hard choices a man has to make in the world. He told me there would be people who would want to use me for their own benefit, not the benefit of my family or the world. For the first time since I met him, he shared a story about his time as a Ranger in Vietnam and his time as a Black Panther here in the States. He had been fighting to insure his family had a shot at everything they deserved as Americans. Jikki told me I would eventually have to decide if I would continue looking for something in my life worth dying for, or if I was courageous enough to begin searching for something in my life worth living for. Until that moment, I did not realize those were actually different things.

We went to court, and although I had not been caught doing anything wrong, the judge stated that since many of my friends had been brought before the juvenile court a number of times, there was no reason for her to assume I was an innocent bystander. She didn't send me to detention as she did the others, but she did put me on probation. She told me that if I got myself together and corrected my behavior and my path, there might be an opportunity to remove those marks from my record at some future date. So, I spent a great deal of time in the next year trying to be better, and I did not spend as much time running around with my friends.

What began to shift my criminal path was my mother's tearful comment on the long drive home when she told me, *"Baby, if you could see what I see every time that I look at you, you would know how great you are."* It was one of those moments when I didn't know who I was supposed to be, but I knew that if she could look at me against the backdrop of all the other things that had been defining me: my disability, my attitude, my place, my skin color, my poverty, and she could still say that, then there was something I needed to look a little deeper for. I think that's when I started to cultivate a sense of hope and possibility. In spite of my reality, there was this picture that was being painted in the back of my mind that would give me a counter image to look at whenever I was about to go over the line.

Lost Again

Before the school year started, we moved to the larger three bedroom apartments near the entrance to Salem South Apartments. I turned twelve in December and was still sharing a room with my brothers. Mom and Jikki finally had a bedroom of their own instead of sleeping in the living room.

The last half of the year, things had been looking up for us. We had an incredible Christmas. It was the first Christmas in a long time when I received separate gifts for my birthday and Christmas. This year, we had everything that Christmas should bring. We had a tree at least seven feet tall that Jikki dragged in late one night. We decorated it with strings of popcorn and penny candy and put a nice blanket beneath it. There were toys everywhere. Both Jikki and my mother were working and things were finally improving. It was looking good for us as a family.

It was a few days after New Years, our break was over, and we still had those great Christmas decorations up. One afternoon, just after we returned home from school, our neighbor a few doors up came knocking on our door, as loud as he could. I was in the back cracking a coconut we were going to eat to celebrate Jikki's birthday. The man continued banging on the door, screaming that there was a fire. I grabbed the little fire extinguisher Jikki kept below our kitchen cabinets.

I ran a few doors down and into the kitchen of our neighbor and saw a spreading fire. The mother had been preparing dinner, and the baby had started crying. She had left the kitchen to check on the baby, and apparently, the grease in the frying pan caught fire and went from the pan onto the cabinet above the stove. We put the fire out on the stove and on

27

the cabinet, but it had already made it to the interior walls. Since these rent controlled apartments were not required to install firewalls between units, the fire quickly spread through the wall and into the roof. Minutes later, it had spread even further and had turned into a huge three alarm apartment fire. As fire and rescue vehicles began to make their way to the apartment, we stood outside in shock and horror, watching as everything we owned went up in flames.

Rodney's mother had been working a number of jobs, and had rented new living room and dining room furniture for the holidays. Rodney's little sister ran out of the building screaming, and we kids decided that if we couldn't save everything, at least we could save this furniture. All of us pitched in and we managed to remove all of the furniture from Rodney's home, depositing it on the front yard of the apartments.

My baby sister, Shawnta, then ran back into our apartment for the Jell-O, obviously because she thought it was very important that we rescue that Jell-O. We also managed to get some of the most important papers, some of my mother's writings, and some of the family pictures before everything else went up in flames. As I sat and watched, I imagined that this could once again turn into an opportunity for a new chapter for me. *"Maybe like the phoenix,"* I thought, *"you have to burn down before you can rise again."*

For the next few weeks, we stayed in other people's apartments and homes. We went to school in other people's clothes. We had to swallow down our rage and embarrassment when someone would say, *"Hey, I remember that shirt. That was the shirt I got for Christmas two years ago,"* or *"Those used to be my shoes."* I tried to be thankful because I was thankful, but it hurt very much. My mother had to split us up again, dividing us among friends until she and Jikki got us resettled. I moved in with Gerald's family and continued going to Brookview Elementary.

We were among the ten families left homeless by the fire. We lost all our possessions. Thanks to the Red Cross, The Salvation Army, and with help from our friends, we were able to move back to Atlanta into an older home in the West End that had space heaters instead of a furnace. We didn't have a lot of anything for a while and slept on pallets on the floor.

CHAPTER THREE

HOPE ON THE HORIZONS

"If the child is not learning the way you are teaching, then you must teach in the way the child learns." Rita Dunn

Something Different

When we moved to Atlanta, I didn't want to attend a sixth elementary school. So, I stayed at Brookview where I was finally finding some confidence and success. I earned a role in the upcoming Valentine's Day play, which opened my eyes to more possibilities. Even though we no longer lived near the school, I received permission, due to the circumstances of the fire, to finish my seventh grade year at Brookview. It meant that at thirteen years old, and for the rest of my seventh grade year, I had to get up at 5 a.m., dress, and take a two-hour bus trip to school.

The next year, my mother told me she was going to enroll me in an alternative school where my differences might not make me stick out as much. From what I understood, that meant I was going to a special school. This "new opportunity" did not appeal to me, but I did trust my mother. I didn't believe that after the fights she had waged against school after school for exiling me to closets or the hallways that she would send me to another box to live out my existence. So I put my faith in her as she took me to meet Lorraine at Horizons School, an inner city, private alternative school.

It took me a long time to realize I was actually attending a private school and my mother had made an arrangement with Lorraine to work for the school in a number of capacities: fundraising, marketing, whatever she could, in order to gain my entry. I think that was probably one of the greatest silent blessings I ever received, another one of those great gifts I attribute to unconditional love. I should not have been surprised because my mother was the definition of a Hope Dealer—she never gave up on any of her children, also encouraging us to try one more time while assuring us of our brilliance.

My first year at Horizons, I was one of sixteen students. Among our numbers were children whose parents were artists and children from wealthy families living in Sandy Springs. There were also punk rockers, skinheads, good old boys, redneck country boys, ghetto boys, and city slickers. We were a very eclectic group. That is what made it so exciting; we had this diverse group of young people who didn't look, think, act, or talk like one another. We definitely didn't have the same life experiences and we were charged with the unique opportunity to build a community. It gave me a chance to witness, and to sample, other lives and other possibilities. Horizons would become the most cherished and meaningful educational experience of my childhood, a completely new learning world.

Horizons Alternative School was a unique learning environment, and my first year there was great. The expectations of the school were very high, but not overwhelming. I believed it would help me achieve what it said was expected. I remember, in eighth grade, receiving an ACT Prep Book as our test book for spelling and comprehension; that was a little intimidating. It took me a while to get used to the range of personalities and the idea that the students were responsible and in charge of everything. We had a work-study program consisting of opportunities to remodel the entire school building. We built greenhouses, did face painting at festivals, sold Navajo fried bread and tacos at international food festivals, and did offset printing and screen-printing.

The students were fully involved and often responsible for the success of every one of our work projects. My first experience with work-study allowed me to understand better what it means to have equity in a place, to invest not just your mind and the work of it, but your body and your own physical effort in maintaining it and making it better. A lot of exciting things were going on at Horizons, and it soon became my home.

I grew up at Horizons. We went on regular camping trips, which gave me a chance to be out in the woods where I could run off all the energy that I built up over a day. I could explore, climb, and touch things and not get in trouble. Classes were small with a great deal of small group work and hands on experiences. Even those like me, those with serious challenges, had the chance to shine, be great, and use the skills we possessed. Sometimes, these plusses would turn into challenges as I bumped heads with some of the staff because I saw myself as a part of Horizons, as a leader there. I realized I had the ability to make Horizons whatever I wanted it to be. I loved the idea.

Trust Forward

Lorraine was the Chief Administrator at Horizons. She was a unique woman. Legally blind, she wore big glasses that magnified her eyes,  and every step she took was very intentional and methodical because she had to know where everything was. I always thought of Lorraine as this hippy chick: long hair, glasses, and plaid shirts, who was calm, quiet, and always so purposeful about every movement. Later, I learned that she had spent much of her life standing against oppression and racism, and her soft-spoken demeanor hid her fierce voice for justice. One of the most impactful moments for me at Horizons was the day Lorraine sent for me to come to her office following a series of events in which I had made some bad choices, something I did off and on.

The principal and cofounder of Horizons, Les Garber, and I had our own personality conflicts on occasion. So when Lorraine called me down to her office, I figured it was about time for me to get the speech I usually got, *"I know who you really are, and I'm waiting for you to screw up so I can get you out of here."* I sat in Lorraine's office and waited for her, wholly expecting to be dismissed from the school and driven from my new home. She came in and sat directly across from me in the only other seat in her office. She sat still for a while, intently looking across at me, and then she said, *"I know who you are, and I think that you can accomplish anything that you set your mind to."*

I don't remember the first thought that came to my mind; I was caught off guard. I knew that Lorraine's vision was very poor beyond a couple of feet, so I shifted in my seat from side to side waiting to see if she would register my movements. Her eyes didn't move as she stared unblinking, waiting for a response. I finally spoke up and said, *"You know it's Hasan, right, Lorraine?"*

She sat there quietly for a few more moments, then repeated herself in the same unbroken tone. *"I know who you are, and I think that you can accomplish anything that you set your mind to. All you can do, Hasan, is make a fool of me for believing such a thing."*

That was the first time in my school career someone believed in me unconditionally. It was the first time in a school setting someone told me I was great and dared me to prove her wrong. I heard her telling me I was already great. I thought she was asking me to find the courage to own my greatness or allow my fears to take me back to playing small, with no expectation of doing more, no challenge of reaching higher, no hope of being better. That is the standard that Lorraine set for every student she encountered. I call it "Trust Forward Thinking." She had the ability to imagine people great, and she gave them the opportunity and the tools to scaffold their dreams to meet that vision or lose that greatness. She made it clear it was a choice.

The Horizons model is a great learning model for our school environments in which we have to feed hope to our youth and give them a chance to grow with it or refuse it. It has to be their choice, not ours.

Lorraine set the course for my academic expectations, even if my achievement didn't always follow. She ensured I continued to develop and grow even when I was barely maintaining and allowed me to express my intellect and understanding in different ways, giving me more responsibility, a chance to lead projects, and most importantly, the chance to speak up. Lorraine was an incredible educator and an incredible woman with a great vision for a school which would allow every child to reach his or her own potential, based on one's ability and commitment to success, instead of on some external rubric or test.

Lorraine made sure that I had opportunities to be exceptional in class by making sure there were things I could be successful at. There were times when I was overwhelmed and frustrated with my own barriers to learning. At those times, Lorraine would say something like, *"Hasan, why don't you go out and run around the building a few times as fast as you can?"* I'd happily comply and exhaust myself. When I returned to class, I'd experience 30 minutes or so of clarity; that was amazing. It was like that sinus medicine commercial where all you see is a filmy blurred image, but then they peel it back to reveal a crystal clear picture. That's how it felt for me. I lived in a constant muffled haze, and Lorraine used strategies to help me burn off the haze for a short time so I could be laser-focused.

I remember being sent out of class once during a test, and Lorraine intercepted me wandering the hallway, slowly making my way to the office. She started walking beside me, which made me immediately slow and measure my pace. Then she began this surreptitious conversation asking me questions about seemingly random things. When we reached her office, she said, *"Okay, you can go back to class and tell your teacher that you passed the test."*

I responded, *"Uh, what test?"*

"You just talked about the concepts and shared great insight about the subject, so let your teacher know you passed the test."

One day a week, the math classes would do mental math instead of written math. I loved that because I was an intuitive mathematician. I could always get the answer, but I couldn't figure out how to explain it. So, Lorraine gave me strategies that would settle me enough to stay engaged. Even though most of the time I was frustrated, I knew I'd have an opportunity to share my knowledge. I'd say to myself, *"Well, wait until Wednesday because on Wednesdays, I'm a math God."* A big piece of my struggle was that my ability to read and comprehend was actually high, but my ability to do it in a way that everybody else did was a challenge. At

Horizons, I had the opportunity to learn and share my knowledge in unique ways.

Building Community

Early in my Horizons experience, I became part of the Student Leadership, which held group meetings whenever a problem came up. In addition, each week, we had meetings where the whole student body would sit and discuss the challenges and successes we were having. If there were problems needing to be addressed, we addressed them together and we'd stay in the room until the problem was solved. It didn't matter if it was about students who didn't make it back to school in time after lunch, a problem dealing with neighbors and the way we interacted with the community, or the way we dealt with each other. I remember sitting in our meeting room for hours and sometimes not having many words said as students looked at each other, or looked to the adults, for answers that were not coming. For me, it was a great opportunity to learn to lead and become a self-advocate and a champion for what I believed in.

The concept of a school wide group meeting was a great model. It allowed us to spend a lot of our energy debating the climate and the culture of our own school. By having so many diverse young people with experiences that did not mirror each other in many ways, it gave us a chance to negotiate our survival and our success together.

A few years before her death, Lorraine brought me back to Horizons to speak to current students who were having their own challenges. She reminded me it was in a group meeting that I had once stood and reminded all the students of their responsibility. How fortunate we were as a group of students to be able to create a better way of experiencing our education beyond what was typically allowed in the rest of the world. We were given the ability to create the environment that was best for us, an environment in which we pushed each other towards success. We were able to create that expectation for each other, even if the rest of the world wasn't willing to give it to us.

I suggested that since Horizons was our school, we could decide what was acceptable and set the norm. We could treat each other with respect and support each other, even if we didn't look, think, act, or talk like each other, because we deserved to have that kind of support. We could make it happen. We, as students of the school, could make something better than what we had experienced on the outside, in order to get a successful result we couldn't get on the outside.

Experiences like that made Horizons a deep-rooted part of the experience I had growing up. It was funny Lorraine reminded me of that conversation because in the work I do building community in classrooms and with young people, that is the primary lesson I try to communicate. We do our work together by setting ground rules and building capacity through engagement. The young people I encounter get a chance to build the community they want, so they can learn and grow together as they choose, and not necessarily as the rest of the world dictates.

A Second Home

I met some really special friends at Horizons. This was a great joy for me. These were friends who taught me how to play Dungeons and Dragons and got me involved in going to places and experiencing things I had not experienced before. I had one friend in particular, Johnny, who was younger than me, and a very bright young man. His mother, Patty, and his sister, Alice, were very involved at Horizons. Patty was one of a kind, and had a big heart for children. Since the older guys would let Johnny play Dungeons and Dragons with us at school, Patty began to invite us out to her house on the weekends. We would have three day gaming sessions; it was a lot of fun, and an opportunity to be young people without all the other drama that often goes along with it. It gave me another place to hang out instead of being at home with my brothers or running out to places where I found less positive, more dangerous activities to get involved with. Patty's home became my safe place. For many of us, it was a lifesaver. She was definitely one of my Hope Dealers, and she, Johnny, and Alice became part of my extended family.

As the school continued to grow, it moved from 10th Street to Ponce de Leon, and opened a boarding program. I was still traveling back and forth from home to school on the bus. My brothers and sisters all went to other schools. As I entered my third year at Horizons, I became the first boarding student in the new program. It was especially exciting because, for the first time in my life, I had my own room until my roommate, David, arrived. Even then, I still had my own bed! It was a great opportunity for me to both live at the school and to be a part of such a unique school community.

Reality Check

Once, when I was sick, I went home to visit my mother to see what I should do about it. As she was walking me back to the bus stop, a police car pulled in front of us onto the curb, the officer exited the vehicle with his hand on his gun and ordered me into the car. My mother stepped between us and asked what his reasons were. He told her if she didn't get out of the way, he was going to arrest her too.

My mom is 5 feet 2 inches, but fierce, and she refused to let this officer take me. He finally said he just got a report of an armed robbery with two black men in Army jackets. I had on an Army jacket that I wore often. He looked at the jacket and assumed I must be one of the guys. He wanted to arrest me and kept telling me to get into the police car.

Mama was holding my arm and explaining calmly that I was just fourteen years old and I was not getting into his car. She kept repeating, *"He has been with me all morning."* The cop was getting more and more frustrated when the announcement comes over his radio that the two guys had been caught. Although he had been in the wrong, he glared at us as he pulled away.

That was not the only interesting visit home. My brother, Sean, had an incredibly mechanical mind. He was always taking things apart and tinkering with whatever he could find. He had an amazing curiosity that allowed him to look at something and see what other people couldn't even imagine. He'd take the toaster apart and wire it to the doorbell. He would do all kinds of creative things that would just drive my mother crazy, but he was curious, and I was in awe.

During one visit, I walked into our bedroom and found Sean sitting in a corner on an old wheelchair, with wires wrapped around his head; he was speaking in a low voice. Using his tag, Casanova Lover, because he always had this smooth talk he would use when talking to girls, I asked, *"Hey Cazz, what are you doing?"*

He answered, *"Yo man, I'm talking to my girl."*

I took the wires from him. *"Hello, hello,"* and somebody answered.

"Hello?"

I said, *"Oh snap, Sean, where did you get this?"* It was very cool and I was dumbfounded. I had never seen anything like that.

He laughed and said, *"Remember the old Walkman? I took the Walkman and an old phone, and took them apart. I started messing with the wires and the boards inside until I got some static. I just kept on messing with it and messing around until I finally got a dial tone, so now I can call my girl."*

My baby brother, at thirteen, had built a telephone headset, something that we had seen only on science fiction television, while sitting in his room, so that he could chill in the corner and talk to his girl. I said, *"Sean, you could be one of those electronic guys. Electronic guys do it all!"*

He just started laughing, and he said, *"No, man. This is just what I do when we're hanging out at the house. Ain't nobody gonna let me do this in the real world."*

That's the thing that's been driving me to beat my head against the wall all these years. I walked out of that door, and I could hear Sean's voice in the back of my head, *"Ain't nobody gonna let us do this in the real world."*

I thought, *"Okay, I guess that I'm a little more hardheaded."* On that day, I understood that I might lose Sean, because with all his talents, all of the gifts, he did not think that he had permission, or the right, to imagine himself to be greater, not after his early years..

Expanding My Horizon

While I attended Horizons, my mother also made sure I had the opportunity to learn new skills from other great mentors. The Neighborhood Arts Center was a place that we frequented after school, and it was the hub of our family's activist and artist community social life. Alice worked there as a writer-in-residence. We studied the Northern Chinese Praying Mantis Kung-fu and Ju-Jitsu in the Tabala School of Martial Arts. The teachings and discipline I learned from Sifu Sheria and Sifu Lateef made martial arts a lifelong passion for me. That is also where I met Bill Prankard, a middle-aged white man who was a screen-print artist at the Center who I was pleasantly surprised to have in my life. I started to work with him as a screen-printer's assistant and apprentice, learning the ins and outs of professional screen-printing. He was convinced that this skill could get me anywhere I wanted to go in life. He taught me how to print on posters and fabric and even let me contract one or two projects and work on them from concept to product. I learned a lot. Bill Prankard was a man whose life was very different than mine. It was interesting to watch him navigate the world, to see his "privilege" at times, and to see him struggle to be just a regular guy.

One day, I was riding around with Bill in his old truck. He owned and rented out a few apartments, and sometimes I went to help him out with odd jobs and maintenance. We passed a house with piles of old furniture and personal items left on the curb. What I knew, because of my own history and experience, is that those folks who lived in that apartment had been evicted; what was left on the side of the road was what they could not carry. Bill stopped his truck on the side of the road and started to rummage through these things. I was almost embarrassed for him, but noticed that he didn't seem to be concerned about that at all. He look through a pile until he found a stained and dirty old army ammo box; he grabbed it and tossed it in the back of his truck, and then hopped back in. I was surprised by what he had done and chalked it up to the privilege of being an eccentric white man; he could go through other people's trash and not have anybody make assumptions about him. For me, it has always been interesting to learn about the lives of people with different backgrounds from mine.

Surprise Ending

After completing almost five years at Horizons School, and after all the experiences of leadership and opportunity I gained, I eventually came to an impasse with one of my teachers. Les Garber had been a teacher and also part of the leadership and founding group of Horizons. He and I didn't always see eye-to-eye, and there were plenty of times when we bumped heads. I think we both had a passion for Horizons, but we clearly had different ideas about what the school should and could be.

Eventually, I failed one of his classes my senior year. As a result, Lorraine called me to her office, and said, *"On the track that you're on, it won't be possible for you to complete the credits you need to graduate by the end of this academic school year."* Sitting in her office again, in that same seat I had sat in just years before, I was paralyzed, unable to ask for clarification. I stared at her and cried, as she, the first educator in my life to ever tell me and show me that I was great, explained that I couldn't stay at Horizons any longer.

I loved Horizons. It was my whole life, my home. It was what had kept me out of the streets and out of trouble. I so wanted to be the man that Lorraine and my mother showed me I could be. So, when Lorraine told me that I had to leave my home, my friends, and the family I had made of these kids that didn't look, think, act, or talk like me, but who gave me this whole sense of what love and community could do, I was angry, completely conflicted, and breaking down inside. I didn't know how I could move past this. If I weren't to graduate from Horizons, which was the only true educational environment I had known, what would I do?

I believed in Lorraine as I believed in my mother, so if she thought that this was the best thing for me, then I would have to figure out how to make her right. I packed up my things in the dorm room, and said goodbye to my roommates. They watched while I packed, urging me to go and confront Les, and place the blame for my removal squarely on his shoulders. It may have made me feel better, but with hindsight, wisdom, and age, I understand now, that whatever hold Les ever had over me was a hold I had given him. It was something I failed to do, not something he chose to do. I think in my experiences of success and failure, that has become my greatest truth.

In fact, most times, when things didn't go well for me growing up, it was because I did not do everything I could and I left the opportunity for other people who had different ideas to believe whatever they thought was acceptable. So, I left Horizons without confronting Les. I did, however, bust all of my knuckles beating on a refrigerator as I dealt with my frustration and rage. Two of my classmates gave me a ride back to the house. It was funny to watch them, individuals who came from a different part of town and a different socio-economic level, drive through our neighborhood. I gave them very clear instructions on the shortest route out and thanked them for the ride, and for their courage, to roll with me on my last trip from Horizons. I tried to enroll in Atlanta public schools to finish out my senior year, but I was told I would not be admitted back into the public school system. Instead, I began making plans to take the GED in the spring and went looking for work.

Another Brother

While at Horizons, I worked summers at Southwest Montessori School. Joe and Charlene, who were the parents of my friend and classmate Jory at Horizons, operated it. When I left Horizons, I was offered part-time work at the school. It was an incredible school that served a range of young people and families who were from the history books of the Atlanta Civil Rights Movement; it was a very supportive community. I met my best friend, Derrick, while working there during the first summer. We were both hired to be counselors for the younger students and teach a martial arts class together. We ended up on the same bus heading toward the end of the line on our first day of work, and by the time we exited, were the only two left on the bus. Derrick was dressed in pressed shorts, loafers, dress socks, a button down shirt, and shades. I was wearing combat boots, an army jacket, aviator glasses, a bandanna, and a bad attitude. I learned later that he thought I was following him intending to rob him when we got away from the crowds.

Once we got to know one another, we became fast friends. We spent most of our time together on the bus and the MARTA trains, playing video games at the arcade downtown, working with the students, and practicing our martial arts. When we met, he had a girlfriend, a white girl from a different part of town. Her mother and Derrick's mother both frowned on the thought of an interracial relationship and it was almost as tragic as Romeo and Juliet. The young girl's mother committed her to a psychiatric hospital for observation and treatment, and Derrick's mother eventually put him out of their home. So, in the true fashion of my mother, Alice Lovelace, we made more room in our family for Derrick.

CHAPTER FOUR

WHEN ONE DOOR CLOSES

"When bright young minds can't afford college, America pays the price."
Arthur Ashe

What Next

While working at Southwest Montessori, I realized I had to get back on track to complete my high school education and figure out my  next move. I knew there were people who expected that this would be the end of my story, a fitting end for me after all that I had been through. Then, early in the new year of 1985, Derrick's home and school life began to completely unravel, and he was expelled from Grady High School. So, we made an agreement that the two of us would get our GEDs together. Then, we would go to college, get our degrees, and become great thinkers and important leaders. All of those people who doubted us would have to eat crow. Shortly after that, Sean was also expelled. It turns out that none of us, none of the boys in our family, actually completed high school.

Derrick and I took the GED in April of 1985. I had not been testing more than a few hours when I suddenly came to the end of the booklet. I looked around the room at all of the other test takers frantically working through their test books, then saw Derrick playing with his pen, test book closed on his desk. We looked at each other in silent conversation and subtle shrugs and came to the conclusion that, for better or worse, we were done. There were a lot of concerned and confused looks as we handed in our test and exited the room. Maybe we didn't understand the test, but we decided it was as good at it was going to get. Weeks later, we received notices that we had indeed passed the test and would be receiving our General Educational Development Certificates from the State of Georgia. With my GED firmly in hand, an expulsion from an alternative school, a 1.67 GPA, a juvenile criminal record, ADHD and dyslexia, I decided that my next challenge ought to be college.

I initially wanted to go into West Point. I knew my mother, who had been very active in the social justice community, had some access to people like Congressman John Lewis and other officials who might be able to write recommendations to the West Point Academy. I had not thought much about my anti-authority and anti-establishment attitude, so the idea of me going into an environment like the military was almost laughable. No surprise to my mother, I eventually discarded my application.

Next, I considered Berea College. Early in my senior year at Horizons, Lorraine had introduced us to Berea. It was a unique school which would not accept you if you could afford to go to college elsewhere; you literally had to be poor to be admitted. It was what they called a "Work Study" College. At Berea, every student is required to work on campus doing some of the essential jobs necessary for a campus to operate, jobs that would traditionally be done by hired staff in other institutions. That is why it can afford to charge no tuition. Every student receives a full academic tuition scholarship, although student labor could not possibly cover the full cost of education at one of the nation's highest ranked liberal arts institutions. The program provided each student an opportunity to develop a Berea College work ethic that had a reputation in the real world that the students could not even imagine. I was familiar with this learning and labor model, because we also worked for our education at Horizons. I had no problem with hard work.

After she expelled me from Horizons, Lorraine suggested to my mother that I apply to Berea. So, my mother got me an application for this small college in Kentucky that I had never seen. All I knew was that it was in Kentucky, which immediately brought to mind many negative stereotypes. Still, I filled out the free application and sent it in.

By mid-summer of 1985, I had not yet received word from Berea College about my acceptance. I learned that two of my Horizons classmates, Tina and Monica, had applied and were accepted into Berea for the fall. By the time August came around, I realized that school was supposed to start soon, but I still had not received anything from Berea. So, I picked up the phone and called collect. When the campus operator answered, I asked if she could connect me to the Director of the Office of Admissions.

The man who answered identified himself as Mr. John Cook, Director of Admissions. I momentarily froze, not expecting that I would actually be connected to the Director of Admissions, but there he was. I quickly explained to him that I was in Atlanta and had applied to come to Berea, but had not heard anything. I was wondering what the process was because I knew classes were starting soon, and I had not received my acceptance letter.

Obviously, I know *now* that if you do not receive an acceptance letter from an institution a week before classes are scheduled to start, it means you did not get accepted. But I didn't know that I hadn't been accepted, because I didn't know college culture. My mother had gone to a community college and she was exceptionally bright; she later earned her Master's from Antioch University. However, at that time, we didn't have a history or story of college success in our family.

I discovered the great thing about not having a lot of experience with a college environment is that you don't know what you don't know. You don't know that a week before classes start, they've long ago selected all the people they will invite to come to their school. You don't know that if you haven't heard from them, they've probably put your application in the garbage can or in some file that says, "DO NOT OPEN EVER AGAIN." So, not knowing these things, maybe you get the courage to pick up the phone to call for answers.

Mr. Cook was kind enough to pull my file from whatever special cabinet they had put it into and got back on the phone with me. He explained that Berea was a very competitive school with many more applications than the number of student spots available. They only had a few openings to fill in the freshman class, and he was reviewing some very promising applications for final approval. He told me he did not think it was going to work out. I told him I understood and asked him to let me know his final decision soon so that I could make my plans. I hung up the phone still convinced that I would be going to Berea with my friends. About an hour later, our phone rang. It was Mr. Cook. *"Okay, Mr. Davis, I think we're going to give you a chance."* All of a sudden, I was going to be a college student.

Try to imagine what must have been going through Mr. Cook's mind when he called me back and told me that he would be accepting me as a student at Berea. It almost sounded like he was still trying to convince himself that it was a good decision. I know my phone call made a difference. Sometimes the only way for people to know the real you is to make it personal, to separate yourself from what they have learned about you on a piece of paper. I think most people root for the underdog, but they have to have a reason to see you beyond all of the others. When I speak with young people, I always say, *"It is important for you to introduce yourself to the world and to know what you need to be successful, because most people want to help. They like an underdog, but if you don't know what you need or if you don't make yourself known, all they can do is make assumptions."*

A New Adventure

When Mr. Cook accepted me as a student of Berea, everything changed. I had not thought about college in a concrete way, and now it was going to be a reality. I began to pack and let folks know that I was going off to college. Right before I was to leave for school, we had a party. I had gathered all my belongings securely in duffle bags and garbage bags. Bill Prankard, my mentor who taught me to be a silkscreen printer, showed up at the party with this beautiful wooden chest. It was painted steel metal grey, with rope handles on each side, and a padlock on the front. He brought it in, set it down, then said, *"Hasan, today you become a college student, and college students deserve to have some place to put their stuff."* It was then that I remembered the raggedy old box that Bill had found on the side of the road and thrown into the back of his truck. He had transformed that piece of trash into an amazing gift for me to carry into my next adventure. Surrounded by friends and family, it finally sank in. It was an incredible moment! I realized I was going to get to walk on a college campus and begin my next journey. It made me feel I was like every other student starting at Berea; I was there on purpose, not an accidental tourist.

Early Sunday morning, we loaded all my belongings into Jikki's old Gremlin, and took off for Berea and freshman orientation. We arrived in Berea very late after a day filled with calamity. The car broke down in Tennessee and it took most of the money Mom had to get it back on the road. We pulled off Interstate 75 at the Berea Exit just before midnight. It was immediately clear that I was no longer in the city; as a matter of fact, we had not passed anything that looked like a city since Knoxville, Tennessee. The streets of Berea were deserted. Between the highway and the college were two traffic lights, and one of those was a flashing yellow light. I jokingly said it was a caution light, and maybe we should heed it.

I couldn't recognize one store, but saw a truck stop and an all-night diner. When we reached campus, there was no one there to meet us and I had no idea where to go. We drove around campus following signs for the student center. A student on duty at the information desk, preparing to close the building for the night, explained that orientation occurred about eight hours earlier, students got their room assignments, and parents had already left for home.

She called Student Life for guidance. We were directed across campus. At Bingham Hall, the head resident advisors, Virgil and Jackie Burnside, greeted us explaining there were no more dorm rooms left on campus. A few students who also had not received room assignments were camped out in the lounge, in what had been turned into a makeshift dorm. There was room for one more. We moved my stuff from the car to the lounge as I wondered if maybe we should forget about this endeavor.

My mother gave me the only money she had left to spare, $20. She pressed it into my palms and told me it was time to decide who was right about me and who was wrong. *"You have to make a choice."* Those were her parting words to me.

I went to get to know my fellow latecomers. We discussed the possibility that some freshmen would get homesick and drop out so we could get a room. All the time I was hoping that I was not the one who would be calling home. Meanwhile, we still had to get to class, study, and sleep. This is how I began my Berea College journey.

I knew that students had to be poor to even qualify for acceptance to Berea, and every student accepted received a full four-year academic scholarship. What I learned later was that Berea was the first interracial higher education institution founded during slavery in a slave state. Its mission was to ensure that opportunity and access to quality life-changing education was not denied to anyone willing to work hard and earn it. Berea has a wonderful legacy of graduates, many of whom planted the seeds of the justice for the next century. Graduates include Carter G. Woodson, the founder of what today is known as Black History Month. I was excited to make this great legacy mine.

Sometime during my first weeks at Berea, I was assigned a dorm room and a roommate, Marcus. People on campus spoke to me and, instead of greeting them, I growled. I believe now that I was attempting to build a force field around myself to prevent others from targeting me in this new and unfamiliar environment. I made it a point to wear my armor as thick as I could. I had my Army jacket and my aviator glasses; I wanted to dissuade as many people as possible from interacting with me.

I had no idea how I was supposed to operate in this environment. What no one knew was that I still secretly used a third grade penmanship pad to practice my handwriting, and practiced using basic reading and comprehension techniques when I was alone in my room. When classes started, I tested into remedial English and Math. All of this made me feel more like an imposter than ever before. I tried my best to keep up with other students who seemed to be perfect, brilliant, and bright. Each day I returned to my dorm room thinking, *"Oh my God! How am I going to learn enough to get through the next day?"* I kept thinking, *"I talked my way into college and now I have to figure out how to stay here."*

On top of anxiety about my classes, in rural Kentucky, I was far out of my comfort zone. I was without my brothers to support me, without anyone who looked like me, thought like me, acted like me, or talked like me. Since the time I was a kid, my brothers had my back. We protected each other, and I knew that if I made a move to the left, they were there to cover my right.

At first, everyone I met seemed to be stereotypical of what I understood about Appalachia, which came out of the *Beverly Hillbillies* and the movie *Deliverance*. The truth is, I was carrying as many ignorant and exaggerated stereotypes about these people that I did not even know, as I imagine many people had about me. So, I kept to myself as much as I could. I spent some time with my roommate, but I was trying to figure out how to navigate a system I had never prepared myself to be a part of.

Making Friends

I eventually realized my college success would hinge on my ability to forge new relationships with people who appeared on the surface to be unlike me. This was difficult because I arrived at Berea with an attitude that I had to be the big tough guy that didn't speak to anybody. I was smart enough to realize I had to break from this pattern. I began to see people at Berea who reminded me of people from home and from Horizons. Slowly, I started to make friends.

As I grew more comfortable, I realized how much of a people person I truly was and how much I loved the idea of being in this community; it felt like a bigger Horizons. Luckily, one evening I was visiting a new friend in the dorm at the edge of campus, Blue Ridge, and there was an open house. Each dorm held a party during the semester and invited students from across campus to visit, enjoy refreshments, dance, see the rooms, and meet with folks. These open houses were one of our best and largest opportunities to socialize, as very few students had access to vehicles to travel off campus.

As I passed one particular door, I heard a lot of noise and a lot of very, very loud guys laughing and talking. I peeked in and saw a large African American man. He was laughing very loudly, sitting at a desk rolling dice with the other guys. This was something I recognized. No, they were not shooting craps. This was something else that I recognized. They were playing Dungeons and Dragons, the role-playing game I learned at Horizons. I stepped in cautiously, and when they saw me, they acknowledged me as I watched for a while. The big guy introduced himself as Keith Goode and asked if I knew how to play, I answered yes. So, they invited me to roll up a character and play.

Keith became part of my balance; he was someone who had an experience similar to mine. I figured if he was there and making it as an upper classman, maybe I could too. We became good friends, and Keith introduced me to his circle of fellow gamers. Most of them were country boys, and it was great to build a relationship with people who were so different from me. Thirty years later, that loud guy, Keith Goode, is still my best friend, and most of those country boys are the guys I still call on for advice and support.

As I became more comfortable with this new environment, I got involved with other activities on campus. However, I continued to hide the fact that I was struggling academically. I learned early on that there were people who take advantage of your weaknesses. Although Berea offered extensive academic support services, my attitude kept me from fully engaging with the support system available to me. I feared I would be singled out again, and I did not have my mother or Lorraine to rescue me. So, I kept my needs to myself. I struggled to get out of remedial English and math so I could finally call myself a real college student. My academic deficiencies began to show in my grades and made it harder for me to keep up in class.

In addition to falling behind in my classes, I was also behind in my work hours. At Berea, you could find yourself on probation for labor violation as easy as you could for academic failure or not going to Convocation. Ironically, my first job was in the library. Considering my disability and general dislike for books at the time, it was often difficult to get to work. Soon, I found myself falling further and further behind in my labor assignment. This meant I had to stay on campus during Christmas break to make up my hours. I barely survived the first and second semesters; my overall G.P.A. slipped. Towards the end of the spring, I was notified that I would begin the fall semester on academic probation. On a good note, I finally tested out of remedial English and Math.

That summer, I decided to stay on and make a little money working full time and taking a class. I worked on campus with four classmates as part of the grounds crew where I encountered, as an observer, one of the summer youth programs called Upward Bound that brought high school students from rural communities from across

Kentucky to Berea. Most of the students were high-risk, low income, first generation kids; actually, they were a lot like me, except that the majority of them were rural, white, and from my first impression, obnoxious. We had several negative encounters. I couldn't understand how some of my friends could deal with their attitudes when working with them. I knew there was no way I could tolerate that.

Way Out of My Box

In the fall of 1986, I began my sophomore year. Emboldened by the new sense of freedom from my old self, I tried out for the cheerleading squad. Although I didn't have the opportunity to join the team, I would eventually join the squad. Before the end of the semester, the head cheerleader left and they were looking for someone to replace him as a male base for the pyramid. The squad asked if I would join them and I did. I may have been the scariest looking cheerleader in the history of Berea Cheerleading, but I was enjoying the freedom and life outside my comfort zone.

I also signed up for a number of campus-wide speech competitions open to the public headed up by the Speech and Debate Coach Dr. Harry Robie. After I showed up out of nowhere and clinched top prizes in a number of categories, he tracked me down and demanded I pay him back by considering joining his forensics team. My social life began to improve.

At the same time, I was struggling in a number of classes and realized my grades were slipping faster than I could shore them up. I knew I was going to be expelled from school. In trying to hedge it off, I spoke with the Academic Dean. He concurred that it was pretty much a foregone conclusion, so I asked what we had to do. He explained that once the process was completed, I would have to sit out a year before applying for readmission. Dean Hager commended me on my proactive thinking, at least at the end, in trying to find a solution. He said that when I was ready, he would be willing to support my bid to return to Berea College.

CHAPTER FIVE

CHOOSING MY FIGHTS

"If you keep doing what you've been doing, you will keep getting what you've been getting." Unknown

Full Circle

After my expulsion from Berea, I had no choice but to move back to Atlanta. My friend, Keith, had been expelled too, so I invited him to come with me. We moved into the small apartment in the basement of Alice and Jikki's house; this was too much of a cliché to even laugh about. In January of 1987, Derrick, Sean, and a number of other members of the local unit of the Guardian Angels (a volunteer-based vigilante organization made up of dedicated individuals, including inner city youth, who donate their time and energy to help protect their communities), volunteered to protect Hosea Williams and other civil rights activists on a sixty mile march from Atlanta to Forsyth GA, which had been the site of recent racial violence and tension. The two of them, along with several others, ended up needing medical attention due to hypothermia, shock, and frostbite. However, the leader of the organization didn't seem too concerned.

I was once again able to pick up a few hours a week at Southwest Montessori in the after-school program. A few months later, Derrick had grown weary of the work he was doing; it was a round-the-clock job with no pay and the constant threat of harm. The Guardians did receive the occasional charity from a few business or citizens donating food or other items, but it wasn't much. Derrick started working weekends with Sea Breeze, a car cleaning and detailing operation owned by the father of Saun-Toy, another classmate from Horizons.

I was trying to save some money and move out of my mother's basement, so when I got an opportunity to do some janitorial work for Sea Breeze, cleaning up bars and restaurants after closing, I jumped at the offer. The combination of jobs gave me honest work and money in my pockets, but it was clear I was going to have to do more. I also realized that staying in Atlanta was going to create more problems.

I enjoyed spending time with my brothers, but I recognized they did not seem to expect more from life. I realized if I stayed where I was comfortable, I would never get to where I dreamed I would be. I decided to do something else because I didn't want to end up getting stuck at home or back on the streets. It was very easy to get back into that role of being "that big guy" who can make people do things with a physical threat. I considered joining the army so I could get paid if people shot at me, and I would have forty other guys backing me up. I even visited a recruiter and toured a nearby Army base.

Jikki had a long experience with the military, so he sat me down and explained that I needed to make some decisions before joining the service. He queried me about my desire to serve my country and suggested that it be in a way that would best suit me. Even though I was aware of the negative experiences Jikki had as a soldier in Vietnam, I decided to join. He made it clear that he respected my choice and would always support me.

I returned to the recruiting office, completed my paperwork, and then took the military entrance exam. I was surprised when I scored very high on the test and the examiners wanted to place me in Military Intelligence. There was a bonus of several thousand dollars that came along with such a placement. All they needed, they said, was a background check on my family and me. Since I was not really interested in explaining to them that my stepfather had been a member of the Black Panthers, I had a juvenile criminal record, and my brothers were headed quickly down the wrong path, all of which would probably have made that security clearance and background check a real challenge, I convinced them that it would probably be better for all of us if we moved on to whatever was next. They were perplexed, and I explained that I would like to be in a part of the service where there might be some women as I was thinking about them quite a bit. They said transportation and medical were the two areas where women served most often, and since I was never really into needles, I thought that driving a truck might work out better.

So, I enrolled as a Private in the United States Army and volunteered to become a transportation specialist. Ironically, I wound up at Fort Knox, Kentucky right back in the state I had just left. I wrote a letter to my mother from the Basic Training Reception Area, explaining to her what I had done, and that I would be home whenever the Army allowed me to leave. Thus began another adventure; in the Army -- a new culture.

You're In The Army Now

At the reception Battalion at Fort Knox, KY, I was immediately appointed Barracks Commander, probably because I looked like I wouldn't take any back talk from anyone. Once we arrived at our basic training unit, Echo Company First Battalion, 46th Infantry, I was assigned

to First Platoon, nicknamed Black Sheep. *"Wow!"* I thought, *"They knew I was coming."* I excelled at training and at referrals for discipline. I was often commended as a top soldier and disciplined for failure to properly address my superiors in the same week. However, what I learned as a Squad Leader was that I could, on my best days, hold men together through crisis. I was a good leader when I wanted to be and a great leader when I needed to be.

I finished basic and advance training in December, in time for what was commonly referred to as the exodus, the annual transition of military personnel back home for the holidays. Many of the guys in my unit went home for short visits before their permanent duty assignments.

I was offered the opportunity to attend Officer Candidate School (OCS) or take Special Operations training. Both would have required me to stay on active duty. As proud as I was for graduating at the top of both of my training classes, I was tired of taking orders and had important work I had started and needed to complete. My exodus marked the end of my active duty service and my transition into the Army Reserves.

Refocused

I returned to Atlanta over the Christmas holiday and enjoyed my time with family. For a while, I tried to keep up with my younger brother, Tony, on the social scene. I quickly realized I would never be cool enough to keep up with that crowd and lifestyle. I soon found myself running the streets with Derrick and Sean, and noticed they had both become more disillusioned. They had begun to slip back into a sense of angst and anger about their inability to be more and achieve more. It bothered me that these incredible men, my brothers, my best friends in the world, the most intelligent men I have ever known, could not imagine themselves greater than what they were at that moment.

I tried, without success, to convince Derrick or Sean to think about college, maybe come back with me to Berea. I argued that if we were in school together, we would make a powerful team, and nobody could stop us. Unfortunately, Sean had made it clear years earlier that although he was brilliant, he couldn't imagine someone giving him the opportunity to share that brilliance with the world. Derrick still talked about being great and all the things we could do together, but I sensed he had a real fear that if he tried, he might fail. Rather than fall down again, he would simply not try.

CHAPTER SIX

FACING MY FAILURE

"Persistence and resilience only come from having been given the chance to work through difficult problems." Gever Tulley

Back to Berea

It was January 1988, when I bought a bus ticket back to Berea. My intention was to spend a few days there, talk to the faculty on campus, and see a few friends who I hadn't seen since I left, including a few who had written me in the military. After a couple days catching up with friends, I decided that it was time to pay a visit to Dean Hager's office. I went to his office and re-introduced myself. *"My name is Hasan; I was a student here. I got expelled, but I am ready to come back to school."*

The Dean said that he remembered my name then he explained that re-admission was not a possibility at this time, especially since it was mid-year and spring semester was starting in a few weeks. I thanked him for his time, and told him I would stop by tomorrow. The next day, I showed up at his office and asked to speak to him again. I explained who I was. *"I know you, you came by yesterday,"* he said.

I reiterated, *"I want to get back into school, and I hope you can help me."*

He looked puzzled. *"I told you yesterday that returning to Berea would not work for you right now. Maybe you can apply for next fall semester with some luck."* I thanked him again for his time and told him I would see him tomorrow. Maybe that didn't click with him, until the next day when I showed up. He said, *"Mr. Davis, why are you here?"* That was an easy question to answer.

"Well, Dean, the only thing I have on my to-do-list is to get back into Berea. I realize that this is a special place, and I need to finish what I started here. But to do that, I need your help."

This time he answered me definitely. *"That is not going to be possible."*

I said something that I probably shouldn't have, but I'm glad I did because it was the way I felt at the moment. I called Dean Hager a liar. I didn't do it with spite; I said it as a fact. *"When I left, you told me that when I was ready to come back to school, you would be ready to support my return."* What I know now is that most people who fail rarely go back to the site of their greatest defeat. They move on, they change the story, they pretend it never happened, they create another story altogether. They go on to some other school; they go on to some other life. They rewrite the story, and nobody ever knows about their difficult moments. The fact that I came back was an anomaly.

I do believe that when he originally said it, Dean Hager completely believed he would be there to support me. However, how many students actually come back after they have had a humiliating failure like mine? I reminded him of our last conversation and his promise to me. He told me he would see what he could do. This time, he suggested I come back the next day. Of course, that was already on my list of things to do.

When I returned, he told me the Scholarship Committee met and decided they would allow me readmission into Berea for the spring semester. He warned me that I was being placed on every type of probation Berea had: academic probation, labor and social probation, even convocation probation. I would be watched closely, but I would be in school. I was very excited. I hurried back to Atlanta, packed all my belongings, and got a ride from my brothers. I returned to Berea ready to start my second term as a freshman.

Back on Track

I enrolled in Freshman Seminar again and began to finish up the class work that I had missed. My success in the military gave me the confidence to return to school, but once back at Berea, I continued to struggle with reading, still using the third grade penmanship pad to practice my handwriting. My reading comprehension was actually exceptional when I was afforded enough time to work through the text and focus without distractions. I had been building and working with my visual cues, so reading aloud was especially helpful because I understand cadence; I understand story. My family is full of storytellers, poets, and writers. I could understand the pattern and logical course of a story, so I was able to compensate for my reading skills. After all, I was an actor since my first performance in the 7th grade Valentine's Day play.

I still couldn't read the books easily or quickly in my classes at Berea, so I used the coping mechanisms I had developed while at Horizons. If I had a book report due, I would interview several students I knew had read the book urging them to talk as deeply as they could about the subject of the book. People love to explain how much they know, especially when they think they are smarter than you.

Following our discussion, I would show up for class and immediately ask if I could give my oral report first. My real skill was the ability to make a connection to the book's topic, and to give enough of the facts so people would give me the benefit of a doubt. I was intelligent, and I had great thoughts. I would sit and discuss topics in science, math, and especially history, and I had deep knowledge. Unfortunately, I couldn't figure out how to communicate the information from inside my head in any way other than to talk about it.

At the beginning of the semester, I went to each of my professors. I explained my situation to him or her, as clearly as I could. I voluntarily let them know that I was on probation and needed to know if I was not performing at a level that would allow me to be successful or continue to be enrolled in the class. Every professor seemed understanding about it. One professor in particular told me that he appreciated the initiative, and he would be there to support me and make sure that I was successful. However, in his class, I sometimes found myself challenged. I was pretty vocal in class, maybe even outspoken. It was a Freshman Seminar, so most freshman listened to professors and nodded, and wrote down what the professors said. By this time, I was a non-traditional student, a few years older that the average freshman, with a range of experiences very different from most students' experiences. I found myself engaged in the class differently than my classmates. The professor and I had great conversations. I would chime in, *"I don't think that's right."* Or I would say, *"I don't agree with that. I think this is the way it is."* I was empowered. What I didn't account for was that this professor might see my contributions as disruptions.

Midway through the semester, I stopped in to visit with him and make sure that things were going well. He commended me on my outspokenness, and suggested that I was doing fine in his class. Even so, there were a few worrying incidents. On one of the days I was late to class, he chose to stop his lecture when I entered. He called me out it in front of the class. I was caught off guard, but I kept my composure.

Despite my level of frustration at this incident, I managed to take my seat. I was trying to be a different person, so I acknowledged my contribution to the situation. This incident should have been a clue for me that things were not going as well as I thought.

In the meantime, I had the opportunity to meet Maya Angelou and Alex Haley. (As I described in the introduction, my time in their presence gave me a boost of courage and confidence that I was on the right track.) I was so excited about the direction things were going that I decided to apply to stay on campus and work the next summer. I could hardly believe that I was walking into the Berea College Upward Bound office asking Bill Best and Mary Ellen McLaughlin if they would give me a job working with the same kids I swore I would never tolerate. I figured they could use someone who could shape those rotten kids up. I was riding high thinking I was finally finding my success in classes and on the cheerleading squad; I even let Dr. Robie rope me into getting involved with the speech and debate teams. Things were going so well for me that I thought I had earned a week or so of family time. When spring break rolled around, I bought a one-way ticket home, and headed back to Atlanta to hang out with my brothers.

CHAPTER SEVEN

NOT CHOOSING IS A CHOICE

"Graveyards are full of people who intended to make better choices tomorrow." Hasan David, J.D.

Back on the Block

While I was home during spring break, my brothers and I decided to go to hear my father's new band. Jikki had a reggae band called *One Drop Plus*, and because I went off to school and then the Army, I hadn't had a chance to hear them play. So, I was excited to go to the club and hear them while spending some quality time with my family.

Before we went out, I met up with Derrick and Sean and we fought. Our fighting was a new thing that started the first time I showed up wearing my Berea College cheerleading jacket. My brothers were concerned I might not be as serious, or still willing to do whatever was necessary, if things got hot when we were out together.

"You know you can't go out with that on; we'll be fighting all night."

"But, you know, I wear it all the time at school, and everybody likes it."

"Well, it's fine at school. When you are an egghead college boy, you can do that. But you can't wear that jacket here."

So, I gave the cheerleading jacket to my baby sister, Shawnta. This incident, among others, started our ritual of fighting; full contact, no holds barred. As long as they wanted to swing, I had to be able to keep standing. If, when we were done, I was still standing, I was good to go, and if not, I would have to stay home with Mama. We did our dance and fought hard and furious. When they were done swinging, I was still standing, so they said we were good to go.

Derrick had this old Chevy S10 pickup truck, black with a red stripe down the side. It had no extended cab, just one the long seat that could fit three fairly comfortably. Derrick was driving around Southwest Atlanta, with Sean in the middle and me at the window, trying to figure out why the dyslexic guy was in charge of directions. We couldn't find the club, so we pulled into a gas station, parked, and sat there for a few minutes taking in our surroundings while trying to figure out how to get back on course. All of a sudden, the truck began to vibrate. This furious base was thumping, and a few seconds later, an old 4-door sedan came cruising into the parking lot and glided to a stop. The windows were tinted, chassis sitting low, and all four doors popped open. Six brothers rolled out looking like they owned the place; they were mean mugging, looked over at us across the parking lot before walking into the store.

Derrick shouted, *"Do you see the way those cats looked at us?"*

"No. I'm just trying to think of where the club is."

He saw something because when you're looking for it, you always find it. He threw the truck into first gear, pulled up behind their car, and blocked them in just as they all started rolling out of the store. Since my window was next to the back of their car, I started talking as they approached, *"It's okay guys, you know, we are trying to find this club, go listen to some reggae music. Maybe you can hang out with us; we are trying to figure out where it is."* Clearly, I was trying to use all my college communication skills, but it was not the right place for it. They started going off, going crazy, cursing back and forth, and Derrick was giving as well as they gave. It started to escalate

"We're just trying to find the club." I repeated. *"Derrick, just drive! Let's just forget about it."* Derrick was already invested; his motto was you don't let anybody dis you like that. Finally, Derrick got tired of them disrespecting us, and he reached up and tapped the .38 pistol that he kept on the dashboard to let them know that if they were looking for stupid, we were already there.

Instead of doing what a rational person would do when confronted with deadly force, they looked at the gun and back at us, and they went off again. *"You must be out of your mind to think we're afraid of some .38, you must be crazy!"*

I was still trying to navigate when I realized that I hadn't turned my head all the way around. I hadn't gotten back into the mindset of being at home with my brothers. The entire time, I was trying to navigate this situation, to find a way out of there. I was hoping that Sean wouldn't engage because Sean was one of those wild cards. When we were young, he was always good in a fight because he never asked questions, and he wasn't the kind to stop until everybody was done, which had always seemed to be a great trait -- until now. I was very concerned that if this conflict escalated much more, he was going to get involved. If that happened, it was an entirely new level of crazy to deal with.

I continued trying to convince Derrick, *"Why don't we just drive, man?"* and I told this guy, *"Hey, we just trying to find this club. If you want to come with us, I'll buy you a drink; everything is cool."* Because I was a college student, I was trying to use all those skills I had absorbed. I knew there had to be another way to deal with a problem than just with my fists, which is what I had been doing since I was six years old.

As the words continued going back and forth and with me trying to navigate and juggle the situation, I could feel Sean's body start to hum, then shake. I knew we were getting close to the breaking point. I was trying to keep him from engaging with my own attention jumping rapidly between each player in this unfolding tragedy. *"No, Sean! Come on, Derrick, why don't we just drive, man? I'm just trying to find this club."* I was trying to keep everybody focused on me because it was getting worse.

Finally, Sean had enough, and it was clear because he started pushing up on the seat. If you have ever seen the old Chevy S10, you know the passenger seat tips a little bit at the corner and there is a small storage space behind it. Tucked right behind me in that little storage space was an Uzi machine gun. I was sitting in the seat, and Sean started to push forward on me to get the seat up so that he could remove the machine gun. I pushed back on the seat screaming, *"No!"* to Sean, and *"Drive!"* to Derrick. Then I turned to face the dude screaming in my ear, *"Why don't you help me out here and calm down?"*

If Sean pulled the Uzi out, there would not be any more warnings. Sean would simply start to shoot until everybody not in our car was dead. He believed that was the best way to solve this problem. That's what he learned from his mother and all the people who hurt him as a child, from all his pain that we never really had a chance to understand. I was trying my best to keep Sean from flipping the seat.

All the while, I was thinking about my mama and the call that she might get when she arrived home or when she turned on the news. *"Three boys arrested for murder, news at 11."* It would be a story just like every other night, but this time it would be her boys. Someone would call and tell her that she did her best, and she shouldn't feel badly. It was only a matter of time. I was fighting my brother to keep the seat from tipping forward, trying to make sure that we didn't go any further down this road than we already were. I was focused on him, trying my best to reassert myself as the oldest, as the big brother who shared a room with him for eight years. The big brother he fought with every day of those years because, in his mind, that was the only way I would have the right to tell him what to do. I was trying my best, but I was the egghead college boy now. I was the guy who came home to play hard and then go back to college and hang out with the theatre department and the Ag students at the farm.

Through the screams of those fools behind me, I suddenly heard one of them clearly say, *"I got something for that little .38 of yours, punk."* I heard the back door of their car open; for a split second, I froze because I knew that if that was my car and we were rolling, I would have a shotgun in that backseat. In that moment, everything changed, because as much as I didn't want my mama coming down to the jailhouse to visit her boys tonight, there was no way in hell she was going to come to the morgue to claim our bodies. It was time for me to stop thinking like an egghead college boy. It was time for me to stop pretending I could solve all the problems in the world by talking. I had to get my head into this game.

I took a deep breath, I leaned up on the seat, and Sean quickly retrieved the Uzi machine gun. If you're lucky, you've never heard the charging handle of an Uzi when it chambers that first round. It has a very distinct sound when it locks that first round into place. As the round locked, the scene went into slow motion. Sean arched the machine gun out the window aiming it at our would-be attackers who immediately started to disperse, *"Machine gun, machine gun,"* they screamed and dove to the ground.

The guy who was reaching into the car for his gun backed out slowly with his hands up and turned towards us. I could look straight down the barrel of the Uzi to his chest. Sean's finger slowly tightened around the trigger. I looked at the belligerent loud mouth who had been screaming and cursing in my face just seconds before. Now he seemed much less dangerous; he was no longer a crazed thug. He might have been sixteen, maybe. When our eyes met, he began pleading. *"Please God, don't kill me. Please don't kill me!"*

In my head, I was trying to get right with the fact that I didn't have any choices left. I mean I did everything I could, I said all the right things, I created options, I tried to negotiate another way, and nothing new I learned was useful. If I had to make a decision, if all I had left was the ability to choose who dies, it was not a question. I took a deep breath, and I let go of all my dreams. I accepted, finally, that Sean might have been right the entire time. Maybe the script was written years before we got here, and all we could do was recite our lines. I thought about all the challenges and humiliation I had faced: isolated in the coat room, called stupid, broken, and a mistake, classrooms I got locked out of, offices I was sent to, hallways I sat in, and every time that some police officer stopped me because I was too black, in the wrong place, or too poor. It all made sense in the middle of that chaos; I finally accepted that I may not be able to do anything differently.

But then, in the back of my head, right at the top of that cacophony of chaos demanding I get back on script, I heard it. *"If you could see what I see every time I look at you, baby, then you would know how great you are."* The generous words of my mother echoing along that long ride home from the police station when I was only eleven years old. And then I heard Lorraine, who always found a way to appreciate even the most difficult, the most challenging parts of me, *"I think you could accomplish anything you set your mind to, and all you can do, Hasan, is make me a fool for believing such as thing."*

That night, I had two clear voices in my head countering all of the negative narratives of my life, fighting against all of the incidents and the lowered expectations that were directed at me because some people thought I was less than them. With those two voices telling me something different, I decided they were more than enough. If Mom and Lorraine were brave enough or crazy enough to believe in what was possible for me, then I wasn't done yet.

I took a deep breath and I grabbed the barrel of that machine gun. I turned to Sean, and I became the big brother who shared a room and fought with him every day. For a split second, I was the one who could tell him what to do. I made him take his finger off that trigger. I turned to the boy standing before me. I said, *"Lay down, boy, and you thank God I am not the man I was two years ago, because with what you put me through, you would have never seen another sunrise."* I told Derrick to drive, and we peeled out of there like the Dukes of Hazard burning down the streets of Atlanta, no headlights, three black men in a black pickup truck with a red stripe and no grill.

We pulled onto a side road a few miles later, and sat for a couple of minutes until we finally had the courage to do that nervous giggle that you do when you are too tough to cry, until we could pretend like it wasn't that big a deal. We tried to convince ourselves we weren't in any real danger. We finally found the club. When we went in, we found my mother, my sisters, my youngest brother, my father; everyone was there. I was grateful that we were able to be with them and reconnect with family.

Hanging out at the club, listening to my father's band, and being with my family was an experience that I had longed for and missed for months. That night, it became very clear to me that I needed to make some dramatic decisions. Despite all the celebrating, dancing, and singing, I excused myself to the bathroom. Staring in the mirror, I searched and searched as if my face held the answer to why I had not accomplished what I promised.

When we got back to my mother's house, I packed everything that I owned. The next morning, Mom took me to the Greyhound Bus Station and I bought a one-way ticket to Berea. I gave her a kiss and said goodbye. In that long ten-hour ride, I made a promise that I would not return to my mother's house until I could finally be the man that she had been looking at since she picked me up from the police station at age eleven.

CHAPTER EIGHT

FALLING DOWN

"We all deserve someone who can see us as we might be afraid to see ourselves." Hasan Davis, J.D.

See, I Told You

A few days after I turned in my last paper for Freshmen Seminar, the professor called me to his office and explained to me that he averaged about thirty minutes on each final paper. However, he said, he saved my paper for last, took it to the library, and checked out all of the sources I referenced in my paper. He spent four hours combing through those citations and sources until he found what he said were two sentences that were close enough to an original text he felt comfortable charging me with the academic crime of plagiarism, thus failing me in the class. This meant I was in violation of my probation, and that precipitated another expulsion. There was no malice in his voice; this was just a matter of fact. I was dumbfounded and shocked by the idea that someone would actually believe so deeply in a student's guilt he would spend all his energy and focus to prove he was right.

The reality is, as I explain to the young people I work with, there will always be people who make an assumption about you, and they will do everything in their power to confirm they are right. I mean, who doesn't want to be right? Unfair or not, the only way you combat that is to work hard to be exceptional in those moments so they don't have the ability to confirm what they think because you failed to step up. I don't think that it is fair, but it is the reality when you have challenges, when you come to the world differently. Sometimes you have to put in the extra effort. Having this knowledge up front gives you either an excuse to fail or the persistence to continue and to work harder. You have to own that your reality is a little different from others.

When I asked the professor why he decided this was something he needed to pursue in this way, he said it was mostly because of my thesis; my opening statement of the paper was so good, so sharp, and so clear he was convinced I must have lifted it from some other source. I asked him, *"So now, what do you think?"* He admitted it was a very good thesis statement. Then he reminded me there was still the matter of the two sentences; he still felt the need to report me for plagiarism.

Time to Choose

I was at a moment of crisis in my own consciousness, in my own journey. Having worked so hard to try and finally get things on track, this felt like a setup; it felt like I had been targeted. What I know now, and what I have been able to accept, is that I opened the door just like I did at Horizon. I opened the door and allowed myself to become complacent with the idea that somebody else was more responsible for my success than I was.

I don't know what set him on this course; perhaps he thought I was a loud mouth, or a jock, or whatever - just fill in the blank. The bottom line is he decided I was not the right material for his teaching environment and was given the ability to confirm his belief. He thought he saw whatever scheme or scam I was playing on the world, and decided that I did not deserve to be at Berea.

I sometimes think about this encounter. I reflect on it now with all that I have learned about how our minds work. When I am with other champions for children, we talk about the need to believe in possibilities outside of our expectations, the need to stay open to a possibility different from what we have seen. After all, if you can't imagine something different, you look for ways to confirm what you already believe.

I was devastated. Sitting in his office, I was struck with how few options I had. He explained his reason for failing me. It was a hard moment for me because everything about what I had learned in the street culture I grew up in, where I had to be big, furious, and the ultimate force, screamed out that he was disrespecting me. I wanted to grab him and show him how unacceptable his disrespect was.

The entire time I listened to him, I was battling internally with this sense of justice and the knowledge that if I grabbed him, it would only confirm everything he thought he knew about me. After all that I had gone through to finally decide that this is the world, I wanted to be a part of that now. I wanted to rage, I wanted to show my anger, and display all the frustration building inside of me. However, I was trying hard to walk this new walk. I could confirm everything he and each of my detractors thought about me, or I could find a way to hold my heart together and walk out of that room with my head held high.

I took a deep breath and I put on my best face. *"I could walk out of here with the paper,"* I said, *"and you could fail me in the class for not turning in a final paper. Then I would not have this mark on my record."* I placed the paper on his desk. *"But you do what you feel you must do and I will do what I have to do."* That was all bravado. I was talking very fast, trying my best to get out of that little office before my heart caught up with my head.

As I walked out of his office, I burned inside. My fists were clenched so tightly that I was cutting myself with my nails while trying to keep myself contained. I was angry, and the only thing that I could hear was Sean's voice echoing through my skull again. *"Nobody is going to let us do this in the real world."* Nobody is going to give us permission to be great, to be different. All we get to do is what we've always been expected to do. We don't get to transform, we don't get to be something else. We get our script, we read it through, and we stay on it.

Line in the Sand

With that epiphany, I decided maybe it was time to go back to what I knew. My mental to-do list was: apologize to Dean Hager, finish my paperwork, pack my room, call my brothers, get back home, stop faking, and stop pretending. It was time to do what I had to do: hit the streets, be the big guy on the corner, take what I have to take until somebody bigger, badder, faster, and stronger can take it from me. Thus ended the lesson I had been refusing to learn for so long.

I went to see Dean Hager. He had already been notified. I apologized because he had invested a lot into getting me back and giving me this opportunity; I felt I had failed him too. Afterwards, I walked across campus to my college post office box. There was a paper bag envelope crammed inside. Inside was a bandanna wrapped in plastic. I always wore bandanas; that was my tag. I was known for cool, crazy bandanas. This bandana had a Rising Sun with Japanese characters on either side. Written in marker on the cellophane that covered it was the inscription: *Inevitable Victory for Hasan. With love, Mom.*

She had to have mailed it five days prior. We didn't have UPS or FedEx then. For the past month, I had become that evasive elementary school boy who did not want to worry his mother. I had answered all her questions about my progress with, *"Everything is great. I am getting things turned around now. No, really I'm good."* She deserved not to worry about me anymore. So here I was, on the wall outside of the mail room with my expulsion papers in one hand and in the other, my mother's affirmation, reminding me that she has learned to listen to my heart, not my words.

So, she sent me this message: *Inevitable Victory for Hasan. With love, Mom,* which I interpreted as saying this chapter is not closed as long as you're willing to get up again. I sat there in the spring rain with these two messages weighing in my hand like a scale, measuring which carried more weight. I remembered my first night as a Berea College student when my mother put her last twenty dollars in my hand and told me that it was time for me to decide who was right about me and who was wrong. Her prophetic voice echoed, *"You have to make a choice."*

I had a decision to make. I sat on that wall for an hour in the rain thinking about what I had put my mother through and realizing she was still willing to invest her energy in me; she was determined to see me as victorious against anything life threw at me. I recalled the day she picked me up from the police station. If she could still believe in me, then the least I could do was explore a way to turn my situation into success. I decided. When I stood up, I was not filled with rage or embarrassment. Maybe for the first time since meeting Dr. Maya Angelou just a few months before (as I related in the Introduction to this book), I felt hopeful and blessed to have another fight to wage. I completed my exit paperwork, packed, and left. I knew I could not go back to Atlanta.

Instead of calling my brothers to come and get me, I went back and talked with the staff at the Upward Bound office. I shared that I was no longer a student. I understood that this was a program about getting young people excited about completing school and going on to college, or some other opportunity that will change their lives. I was probably not the best example of that since I had just gotten expelled from college again and was expelled previously from an alternative school. *"But,"* I said, *"I want to do something important, and the more I think about it, these kids are a lot like me. I want to be useful here. I want to show them what we can do when we don't give up."*

So, I was given permission to work for the Berea College Upward Bound Program as a Tutor Counselor. I for the next two months I would live in the dorm with the students. I was given permission to move in early, which was good, because until the program started, I would be homeless.

CHAPTER NINE

PICKING UP THE PIECES, AGAIN

"I did then what I knew how to do. Now that I know better, I do better."

Dr. Maya Angelou

Behind My Mask

Even though I was no longer a student at Berea, in my heart, I was still very much a part of the Berea community. I was excited about the opportunity to remain on campus through the summer with the Upward Bound Program. I was happy to have a job, a dorm room, and access to the dining hall for three meals a day. I figured the work of a Tutor Counselor could not be much more difficult than my work at Southwest Montessori and I was on track for an easy summer before deciding what I was going to do in the real world.

All my plans of floating through the "summer camp" disappeared on the first day of our staff training retreat. Director Mary Ellen McLaughlin passed out papers about working with adolescents and understanding these young people; she wanted us to better understand our charges. As I joked with other students about what we'd be learning, one piece of paper in particular caught my eye. It read, *"Please Hear What I'm Not Saying"* by Unknown, a poem by Charles C. Finn. (I recently contacted Mr. Finn, and he gave me permission to reprint the entire poem here, but I recommend you should go to his website: http://poetrybycharlescfinn.com/pages/please-hear-what-im-not-saying to read it for yourself. It is definitely worth it. The poem begins:

Don't be fooled by me

Don't be fooled by the face I wear

for I wear a mask, a thousand masks,

masks that I'm afraid to take off,

and none of them is me.

Pretending is an art that's second nature with me,

but don't be fooled, for God's sake don't be fooled.

I give you the impression that I'm secure,

that all is sunny and unruffled with me,

within as well as without,

that confidence is my name and coolness my game,

that the water's calm and I'm in command

and that I need no one,

but don't believe me.

With those words, I was exposed, laid bare. This was a poem that spoke to my twenty years. These words, and the rest of the training during the retreat, reinforced the vision of Bill Best and Mary McLaughlin, longtime early directors of Berea's Upward Bound program. They feel we are here to serve, making life better for young people who others often think are beyond their care, below their gaze, or beneath their station. So it began. I worked with and fought for those same kids I had described as obnoxious, kids who were mostly white from rural Kentucky, who were labeled high-risk and most likely to drop out of school. Only now do I realize my first reaction was more about seeing so much of myself in them than about them as individuals. These young people, most of who had never been away from home, came to live on Berea's campus for six weeks. While outwardly most of them were unlike me, my connection to them was the experience of being marginalized. I became their fearless champion. I told them the truth, *"I got expelled again, guys, but you better believe next semester I will be back in school."* That was our story, our joke.

Working for Upward Bound was the greatest thing to happen to me at Berea. It gave me a chance to meet a group of young people and find the courage to speak for them, encourage them, and believe in them in ways I had not believed in myself. It was a great way for me to start the practice of giving back. It is where I started to believe that I could be a role model; I, too, could become a Hope Dealer.

Sharing My World

My most memorable experience of that first summer was a late night knock on my door, well after lights out. As a Tutor Counselor, I was always on duty. I opened my door to find a thin, pale young man at my door. He was a quiet, but engaged, member of my Wolf Pack, the designation I gave my group. He was involved in activities we planned and enjoyed the new experience of campus events. I taught him the electric slide and he taught me the "boot scootin' boogey." He danced a little at our weekly dances and had a warm laugh when you could get him to stop looking so serious. I asked if everything was okay, and he just shrugged as his eyes began to water.

"I've been talking to my dad," he started, *"and ever since he let me come up here, he has been warning me to look out for you. He says I can't trust you, and there is no way a black guy can really want to do something to help me."*

"What do you think?" I asked after a long moment of silence.

"I'm not sure. I just need to know if you are lying to us or if I need to stop calling my daddy." I really could not find a good response if those were the only choices.

"How about this? You can ask me any question about anything you want to know, and I will answer the best I can. When you are done, you can decide." We went down to the lobby and talked for a long time. Somewhere in that long conversation, he finally showed up and was present. Maybe he started believing, like I did, that this was a special place. For a short time at least, we didn't have to wear so many masks.

Stronger Together

At the end of the summer, when Upward Bound was complete, I moved to Richmond, Kentucky, which is about fifteen miles north of Berea. A couple of my college friends, one my former roommate, lived in a small apartment. I moved in and took a job working construction. I continued to report for Army Reserves duty each month, but inside, I was holding on, just trying to bide my time. I knew I couldn't move back to

Atlanta or I'd never make it back again. I began dating a woman I worked with that summer in Upward Bound and a few days a week, I went over to Berea and taught self-defense and martial arts together with the head of security. I kept myself involved and made my presence known on campus. I went out once or twice a week with some of the college students, so I wouldn't lose touch completely.

That winter, I got a call from Derrick. He was very vague, saying he was in some trouble and needed to get away for a while. I told him he was always welcome, and I would do all I could to help. So he came up to Richmond, KY and I moved him into the apartment. I introduced him to many of my friends. Most of them were people he never imagined ever knowing, let alone liking, just like me a few years before. It was great to introduce him to my friends and show him there are people who don't look like you, don't act like you, and don't have your experiences, but who could still be a part of your success. He became friends with guys from Eastern Kentucky Appalachian Counties, where coal mining was king. In fact, many of the people I introduced him to became so close they would stop by the apartment to pick him up when I was at work or busy. They definitely made him feel at home.

I came home from work one day and Derrick was counting hundred dollar bills out on the table in my living room. My first instinct was to box him upside the head for jeopardizing both our futures. Instead, I asked him to explain where he got the money. He laughed and said he had gone next door to the gun store and asked them what they might pay for an Uzi. The ban on automatic and assault rifles was about to go into effect, and apparently there was a high demand. He sold the gun and we used that money to pay our bills and party. We managed to get along pretty well, and Derrick seemed to be adjusting nicely to a very different pace and a very different crowd.

Things were going well. We were hanging out on Berea's campus a few days a week and Derrick was making a lot of friends. He started teaching the self-defense class with Daryl and me, and met many good people. It was nice to spend time together, looking after each other, but not having to look over each other's shoulder.

I continued going about my business, teaching the self-defense class, hanging out with Derrick and my friends, and working construction. We were almost finished with the construction project, and I started trying to figure out my next move. I hoped to go back to work with the Upward Bound program for the next summer, especially if I was admitted back into school. I thought it would be a great way to reconnect and get back into the groove.

Taking Different Roads

I returned to our apartment one day to find Derrick in the living room loading black rhino rounds into his .38 pistol. I asked him what was going on. He said, *"The last few months have been the most peaceful I've had in a long time. All of your friends, the love they show me just because I'm your brother, that's crazy! Now I see why you stayed here. This has been great for me. I mean, I haven't been at peace like this or slept this well in, well, forever."* I could feel my throat tighten as I waited for the "but," and it came. *"But, Dawn is going have my son and a man ought to be able to take care of his son. So, I've got to go home, and I've got to be that man, whatever it takes."*

We argued about his leaving. I told him these people were not just my friends anymore; they were his friends too. I challenged him with the idea that if he stayed, maybe when I went back to Berea, I could get him admitted. The two of us could do anything together, and we could do more than either one of us could alone. We could watch each other's back and conquer college, like we had conquered so many other obstacles we faced, together. *"Stay here, get into school. Bring Dawn and the baby here. Learn how to live a good life."*

He laughed at me, and answered, *"Sean was right about you, always trying to find simple solutions to hard problems. Sometimes it just ain't that easy."* Well, that set me off. I attacked Derrick, and it turned into a straight up brawl. When we were done, there was broken furniture around the living room and the apartment was a mess; we left holes in two walls and knocked everything off the counters.

Derrick still had that determined look on his face, but for the first time, I saw what it really was. I saw the fear in his eyes. It's a fear of walking in a different world where you don't know the rules, and you feel like an imposter with a GED pretending to be an egghead college boy. It's a fear of what might happen if a man removes his mask, puts down his weapons, and exposes the dreams that he has never spoken aloud. I recognized that fear because it was the same fear that I swallowed down daily since coming to college. It was the fear that whispered in your ears, *"What if you embrace this world and it rejects you?"*

As much as I love my brothers, as much as I was willing to sacrifice for them, including my life, I finally realized that I could die for my brothers, but I could not live for them. I could not drag them kicking and screaming into the world I thought they deserved. All I could do was be sure they knew there was another world, and hope that the path I was blazing was bright enough and clear enough that if they made the decision to follow, it would be easier for them than it was for me.

A friend from Berea was driving to Atlanta for a photography conference. I asked if we could get a ride with her. When we got into Atlanta, we dropped Derrick off. I gave him a hug and a kiss, and we said goodbye knowing we were about to take very different roads. Then we repeated what we always said when we were not going to be together for a while, *"Take care of you for me. Look after yourself because I won't be there to look after you."*

CHAPTER TEN

THIRD TIME'S A CHARM

"Only those who will risk going too far can possibly find out how far one can go."

T. S. Eliot

Shoot the Moon

After dropping Derrick off in Atlanta, I returned to work and focused on problem-solving how to persuade the college to let me back in for a third time. I had stayed in touch with several professors and staffers who, in the past, had been my supporters. One of those individuals was Virgil Burnside, the same man I met my first night in Berea who found a place for me in the dorms. Virgil was a Berea graduate, an African American man whom I closely identified with over the years. He was always fast to offer his support and encouragement even though I often thought I didn't need it.

Virgil urged me to not give up on returning to Berea, so I made an appointment to meet with Dean Hager. I wanted to let him know that I was ready to come back to school. He was polite and seemed sincere when he told me he wasn't sure that was going to be a possibility, which made perfect sense to me. However, I didn't back off, and asked for a chance to go before the Scholarship Committee. I needed to know I had done everything in my power to make my case as clearly as possible. After that, I was willing to live with whatever decision they made.

Dean Hager arranged for me to meet with the Scholarship Committee, which handled appeals of student expulsions and re-admittance. I knew I was in a difficult position to be trying to negotiate. It's not like their decision to let me in would earn them another freshman paying $20,000 per year as long as Mom and Dad could write the checks. Every time they let me return, it was at the loss of some other student who might have made it through without as much difficulty in four years, an experience that could potentially have changed the trajectory of a life, and maybe even a family's life.

So, it was not lightly that I went in with my request. For the most part, I had hidden my disability from Berea, pretended to myself that it wasn't a problem. I had allowed my challenges to get in the way of my success. I decided it was time for me to put all my cards on the table. I thought about what I should say; it all came down to a very simple conversation. I told them no one is going to look at a place like Berea that gave a man like me three chances, and imagine it's a terrible place. I asked them to consider, what if I make this work? I assured them if I could make Berea work for me, it would support the truth of everything Berea stood for and would allow me to prove to others my ability to succeed. I asked for one more chance to finally get it right.

Looking around the room at their expressions, I could only imagine what they were thinking. Take a third chance on me after plagiarism charges and being expelled twice? Not likely. I still had to ask the question aloud so I would know I had given this opportunity my best. I told them, *"If you take this risk against all logic, I promise to give you my best."*

After I asked them as clear as I could to take another chance on me, I thought I might as well shoot for the moon, so I added, *"And I need you to loan me $3,000 to purchase a Macintosh computer."* As they regained their composure, I explained the new word processor program for the Macintosh computer had a program called spell check that would review my documents for errors while I typed. I believed with such a tool, I could finally get what was inside of my head out in a way that would help other people see what I truly knew and understood.

I left unsure of their decision, but not long after, I was contacted by Dean Hager who told me the committee had decided to honor my request for a third try at Berea. The committee also decided to recommend that the Financial Aid Office find an appropriate loan to help me purchase the computer. Dean Hager made it clear that nobody else on this campus full of poor students had his or her own computer. I realized they really were taking a leap of faith on my behalf. So once again, I was put on every type of probation and told that if anything went wrong this time, I had to promise to just leave. I thought that was fair.

So in the fall of 1989, I enrolled in Freshman Seminar for the third time. One reason I felt so good about this third attempt was that I had found someone I cared deeply about and who believed in me unconditionally. This relationship made me more confident about my ability to succeed.

Lost and Found

I never thought I'd find a partner like Dreama. We met in 1985 as freshmen. Berea was a very small college, so everybody knew everyone else. Although we weren't in the same social circle, we usually wound up at the dances, the weekly open houses, or at O'Riley's on Wednesday nights when Berea College students went to Richmond to hang out and party. We danced at school parties, and sometimes I asked her to dance at the club. Dreama would always say, *"So and so"* she came with didn't like it when I asked her to dance, and I always responded, *"You know, when 'So and so' tells me that, then I might stop asking you to dance."* Or, I'd go sit at her table and take a sip of her drink.

She would say, *"'So and so' doesn't like when you drink the drinks he buys me."*

Again, I'd respond, *"When 'So and so' says that to me, then I'll consider it."* It was just a silly, flirtatious thing.

We were definitely from different social circles. Dreama hung out with the athletes and academics, and I ran around with the gamers and theatre people. During my first summer at Upward Bound, Dreama's best friend, Judy, worked with me. That's how Dreama and I got to know each other a little better; she'd come and hang out on Judy's days off and we'd all end up spending time together by the end of the summer.

The summer of 1989, I returned to Upward Bound. Dreama also worked there that summer and we got to know each other even better. There were, though, several obvious challenges interfering with our relationship. For one, I had a girlfriend. Another was that Dreama was very concerned about her family's reaction to me. Dreama is white and she once told me she had been warned and threatened by some of her friends against dating me. I thought it was comical, not understanding how deeply this concerned her. Sometimes when we took a walk, people would stop their trucks in the middle of the street and stare at us. I guess it disturbed them that I didn't turn around or run away when they did this. Instead, I'd usually approach the car to ask if they needed assistance, and they would speed off.

We separated at the end of that summer. Dreama was on her way to law school and I had to concentrate on making my third college attempt a successful one. When we parted, we mumbled something about seeing each other at Homecoming. I assumed our relationship was over. A few weeks later, Dreama showed up. She said that she had made up her mind, and she was willing to get involved with me. Whatever challenges came with me would come and she felt she would not lose herself in the process. That was a surprise, since I could hardly manage the craziness in my own life and couldn't imagine how she would cope with it.

Dreama surprised me even more when said she felt there was something special about me, and was willing to stick around long enough to find out if we could make it work. This was new for me. I'd heard it in previous relationships, but I avoided deep entanglements so I could walk out tomorrow if I wanted to. This was definitely different.

Dreama is an only child, an introvert who prefers one-on-one relationships. I come from a large family, am an extrovert, and love being with a crowd. This meant that during the week, I'd hang out with my roommate and my friends. On the weekends, Dreama and I would hang out. She could deal with having somebody else in her space for a couple of days, and I could deal with having only one person in my space for a couple of days. That became our norm.

Like me, Dreama grew up in poverty, although she experienced a different struggle growing up in rural Kentucky. She lived in the same house until she went off to college and I remember her being very upset when her parents decided to move into a new house after she graduated. The unique kind of stability she had growing up provided her with the ability to be successful. Neither of her parents went to college, but both were hard-working providers and great supporters of her. In my eyes, the willingness to help your child get something you can't achieve yourself is truly wonderful.

Although we came from such different backgrounds, we formed a great support system for each other, which led to a more meaningful relationship. I was of some help to Dreama in her transition to law school. She didn't enjoy the experience and tired of the sometimes petty competition that went on, and considered dropping out more than once. It was nothing like the shared experience most students had at Berea. I encouraged her, just as she encouraged me. Clearly, she was academically gifted, but I think dealing with the environment and culture of law school was hard in itself because of her background. I did what I could to support her with that, and was very helpful when it came to the litigation piece. Meanwhile, she helped me stay focused on my tasks and be successful with my new tools and my new opportunity at Berea.

Dreama has a real matter of fact nature. Even when I was going through all of my experiences of loss, and they kept coming, one after the other, she'd just say, *"Well, yeah, you know, that happens. What are you going to do now?"* She was a good sounding board and a good balance for me. She helped me stay committed, and at times refocused me, so I could actually get to the goal that I was trying to reach. Dreama promised she would help me become my better self. I was scared to admit it, but even with all of my fears of close relationships, I wanted to believe her.

CHAPTER ELEVEN

THE FINAL STRETCH

"The only place you will find that 'Ability' comes before Opportunity is in the Dictionary." Hasan Davis, J.D.

Fired Up!

Over the course of the next three years, my college life was composed mostly of books and study. With a new computer and spell check as my tools, and Dreama helping me strengthen critical study skills, my classes began to click. The computer ensured my papers were readable and demonstrated the depth of my intelligence. For the first time, I was fully engaged with college life. I felt great about my return.

My first semester back, I made the Dean's List. By the end of the year, I was off all probations. My speech and debate professor, Harry Robie, coached me to a national qualification in speech and debate. I declared my independent major in Oral Communications and focused on theater and speech classes to fulfill the requirements. In my senior year, I was voted Homecoming King, elected President of the Student Body, and honored with the Navy V-12 award in recognition of my contributions to campus life and international kinship.

I even enrolled in a high level Philosophy Coarse taught by the professor who failed me in his Freshman Seminar Class. It was stimulating and provocative. That class, along with a Business Law course I decided to take, provided me the foundation of a strong analytical model and prepared me for the law school entrance exam when I decided I would shift my focus from theater to law.

One of the great things about my last year at Berea was that I found support from what they now call Disability Services. I also received amazing support from my professor in my senior requirement class. Once I explained my challenges and needs, he took it upon himself to meet with retired college faculty and staff along with members of the larger community to recruit volunteers to read all the books assigned for his class onto audio cassettes. He presented me with several boxes of cassette tapes. I was deeply touched by their willingness to contribute so unselfishly to my success.

Not Done Yet

I would be wrong to leave the impression that I did not have any struggles upon my return to college this time. Over the next three years, a number of my cousins were murdered in St. Louis. Each summer, my Upward Bound experience was interrupted by a late night call and a weekend drive for a somber celebration of life cut short. I witnessed St. Louis slowly eating its young, and all I could do was silently thank my mother for courageously planning our escape.

It was important for me to have my Upward Bound students to return to after each of those funerals because I could transform my hurt and frustration into a recommitment to ensuring that other young people got a chance to break their own cycles of trauma, drama, and pain.

In my second year back at Berea, I received a late night call from Sean. He reported Derrick had become involved in an altercation that ended with an angry man shooting into the crowd. Derrick had been hit and then someone threw him into a cab. At the time of Sean's call, it had been a few hours since the incident and no one had been able to find him, not in the local hospitals, or at the morgue.

My heart fell. I was torn between the logic of staying where I was on track to finally affirm the many who sacrificed to give me so many second chances, and the loyalty of family and friends who had been my lifelines on my most difficult days. But, I was still the oldest, and if Derrick did not surface soon, I felt it was my duty to find him. I pulled my "go bag" from the back of the closet, called the bus station to ask the cost of a one-way ticket to Atlanta, and then went to say goodbye to my friends. Before I left my apartment, I received two calls, first from my mother, asking if I had heard the news and just "making sure you are still in Berea." I promised that I was, but left off the "for now" echoing in my head.

When I hung up, I sat for a while in silence trying to figure out why I should not take that bus ride. Then the phone rang again, and it was Derrick calling from a hospital; he explained he had been shot several times, one bullet was still lodged near his spine. *"As soon as I gained consciousness, I had to call and let you know.*" He paused, "*Hasan, I am a grown ass man now. I can't keep asking you to drop everything you are doing in the world every time I screw up my life. That is not how friendship is supposed to work, so I need you to stay in Kentucky this time. You can't keep trying to save me. I need you to be better than that. You need to stay right there so you can show the world what we all could have accomplished.*"

As the phone line went dead, I sat silent, tears rolling down my face. My heart was full of anger, fear, and gratitude. He had just released me from the destructive cycle I had not been able to see for myself. All this time, I thought the definition of friendship was someone who was there for you no matter what, someone who loved you just the way you were, with no expectation of change, growth, or transformation. I thought that as a friend, Derrick needed me to be the big guy in the shadows who only came out when things got bad.

Instead, Derrick released me from whatever obligation I had been holding onto. He wanted me to fly without him instead of risking a fall with him. The difference is knowing what you are willing to live for instead of knowing what you are willing to die for. I threw my packed bag deep into my closet and refocused on my goal.

Looking Back to Move Forward

Graduation was scheduled out on the lawn in front of Berea's Hutchinson Library with open seating to accommodate as many people as possible. The rain site was Phelps Stokes Auditorium, and if it rained, we were allotted only five tickets each for family members. I knew that would pose a problem because although a number of people in my extended family had started college, I was going to be the first in the family to ever graduate. It seemed like everyone in the extended family was coming. So, I began to scramble for as many extra tickets as I could find and eventually wound up with about fifteen. From the number of RSVPs coming in, I was sure my family members would be closer to thirty and they were all planning to witness this momentous occasion live.

I couldn't imagine getting hotel rooms for all of the family members who were coming from St. Louis and Atlanta. I asked the Head

Resident of one of the dorms if she would be willing to let me rent one floor of the residence hall. Turns out, no one had ever proposed that before. So, after a few discussions with Student Life, we came up with a plan which worked out wonderfully. I was excited to have everyone around.

On the morning of graduation, it looked like we would be able to perform graduation on the lawn. By noon, sadly, the weather had turned dark and rain was forecast before the afternoon ceremony. Everyone had to adjust to the much more confined space in Auditorium. There were overflow rooms in other buildings on campus in which the ceremony would be broadcast.

As President of the Berea College Student Body, it was my honor to give the opening welcome and invocation. As I rose to take my position at the same podium Dr. Maya Angelou addressed us from all those years ago, I spotted my mother being escorted down the aisle to take her seat. It was at that moment, as she caught my eye, I realized I was

finally getting a glimpse of the man who she had been looking at since she picked me up from the police station when I was eleven years old.

I stood on that stage, a testament to her and so many other Hope Dealers. It was so rewarding to show her she wasn't wrong for believing, hoping, praying, and fighting all of those systems to create this possibility for me. There was no guaranteed return on her investment of time and tears, but she painted vivid images of greatness for me and for all of her children, so that if and when we chose to gaze upon it, we might find the courage to achieve. Graduation was the beginning of a new vision for me.

When President John Stephenson called my name, I walked across the stage to shake hands with him, the Vice Presidents, and Deans. The Registrar whispered to me as I exited the stage, *"Hasan, you know, we still don't quite know how you did this."* He gave me a smile and a pat on the back. From his tone of voice, I knew he didn't mean that they were concerned that I made it through; instead, my graduating affirmed Berea's core mission - to ensure as many young people who dream big dreams have the opportunity (or in my case, opportunities) to achieve greatness. I believe my experiences at Berea brought to their attention a smaller group of young people who, if served better, could find the same success.

It's exciting to me that today, every freshman student at Berea receives a personal computer from the college upon entry. For many of us first generation, low income college students, this represents a game changer as students get connected to technology that can improve the way they access education and translate it into real success in the classroom and the world. I would like to think that I had something to do with that.

CHAPTER TWELVE

LAW SCHOOL? SERIOUSLY?

"Sometimes it's not enough that we do our best; sometimes we have to do what is required." Sir Winston Churchill

I Decide

During my last year at Berea, I applied to law school. I hadn't intended to go to law school. In fact, my plan was to do more work in theatre; I was told I was a good actor. Previously, a pair of visiting artists from a metropolitan theater company joined us at Berea. After our production, they pulled me aside and said they thought I had the potential to be successful in professional theater. They suggested I choose a graduate program or decide if I was interested in trying my luck in California or New York and they'd be happy to introduce me to individuals who they thought could help me succeed. They were that confident in my acting potential and the conversation made me feel great! I was finally riding a wave of success. Since that first dramatic fall in the 7th grade Valentine's Day play, I had silently flirted with idea of making acting my work. The possibility excited me.

A few weeks later, I was at a party talking about this exciting new opportunity, when one of my classmates chimed in, *"You are a great actor, Hasan, but it's acting. It's not like you could do something that takes a lot of work, like being a doctor or a lawyer."* We argued a while, and I finally walked away in frustration. I knew how much work everyone in theater invested in the passion of performing. It wasn't as easy as many people think. However, I was shaken by the realization that there were people out there who I knew who thought that I was taking the easy route.

I thought I believed I could do whatever I set my mind to, but maybe I was not as secure and confident in the credibility of my recent successes. I thought about my students in Upward Bound. I'd tell them, *"There are no limits to what you achieve except the ones you put on yourself."* With this as the mantra, I had witnessed young adults unlock courage, confidence, and potential that they did not believe they had. Even as I was in and out of school, I always made it a point to let my students know what was going on, so they understood that education was not a destination, but a journey. As long as we have the courage to keep getting back up, eventually there is nothing to do but finally succeed. So, how could I listen to anyone telling me I couldn't do something when I kept telling my students, *"Nobody gets to choose but you"*? If there was something out there others thought I couldn't choose to do and succeed at, I wouldn't be honest in continuing to say that phrase to any student.

I turned my anger over the comment turned into action. The next week, I registered to take the LSAT, the test to get into law school. Dreama, who was in her last year of law school, thought I had lost my mind. I had to take a shot at it; I had to at least see if I could get accepted. I took the test, the results were sent to the three Kentucky Law Schools, and I waited to hear from any of them.

I received a very nice rejection letter from Chase Law School at Northern Kentucky University, then another from the University of Louisville College of Law. I was informed that by order of importance and prestige, I had been rejected by the #3 and #2 rated law schools in the state respectively, so the likelihood of an acting career for me was quickly coming back into focus. However, a few weeks before classes at Berea ended, the University of Kentucky College of Law sent me an acceptance letter. I officially changed course again; it was time to go to law school.

Detour

I was more than a little hesitant about my new direction but determined to make it through. Berea had a great reputation and history of students accepted into UK Law and I had a few classmates starting with me. Before I left Berea, I received advice from a number of supporters. They told me, *"Be sure to find Professor Bob Lawson when you get there. He is a Berea graduate; he will look out for you."* As a UK Law School alumnus, Dreama also shared stories about Professor Lawson. I was excited to know that someone who had become such a distinguished contributor to the UK Law School legacy was also a Berean. Without knowing him, I felt I knew some of his struggle and I was in good company.

I went off to UK as Dreama moved to Bowling Green, Kentucky to begin a law practice. It required even more work and time management for us to stay connected. Dreama, who was the one with a vehicle, was willing to do a lot of driving back and forth to keep us together.

I started law school in the fall of 1992. The student orientation by the upper class was helpful in learning how to navigate the school. I was surprised no one from the Dean of Academic Affairs Office contacted me to schedule a meeting to learn more about my learning challenges and help me create a plan for academic support. My disability was a central theme in my application and the reason why I wanted to study law. My goal was to better serve and support youth like me who struggle to find success in inclusive education settings. I figured with a degree in Law, I could become a disability and youth advocate.

In my application, I wrote about how my use of new technology led to my success at Berea and how Berea had made accommodations for me for additional time to finish my work. Although these accommodations should be provided under the Section 504 of the Rehabilitation Act of 1973 (Section 504) and possibly the Americans with Disabilities Act (ADA) of 1990, unfortunately, I received no offers of support. I knew I was going to need help. Even Dreama had struggled with law school - Dreama, who was such an amazing student! I knew I was going to need all the help I could get.

A Little Help Please

Since I had a disability, I requested assistance from the State Office of Vocational Rehabilitation Services (VR) and was assigned a counselor. I made an appointment to see her to discuss the support I could expect. I was so excited to meet with her; she was my disability advocate, and it was like going to Disneyland after everything I had been through as an undergrad. One wall of her office was nothing but plaques, certificates, and awards. I couldn't even see the wall behind them. As far as I could tell, she must have worked for forty years as a disability advocate; I thought I had hit the jackpot. I sat down, she pulled out my file, and we talked about my history. I told her, "I got accepted to law school, and I'm here. I need to figure out a way to make this work. I've got too much riding on it. I don't really care about practicing law. I don't even know if I like lawyers yet, but I have to get through law school."

My champion was completely empathetic. She sat quietly and considered me for a while as her eyes started to water. She finally spoke,

"Hasan, it looks like you have been failing your whole life." I didn't like the way it came out of her mouth, and I hoped it was just a bad first impression. She continued, *"I'm so afraid that if I support your efforts to graduate from law school, it is just going to end in another failure."* By now, I was at the edge of my seat trying to figure out exactly where she was going with this. She clarified, *"I'm afraid that law school is just going to be another failure for you, and I can't have that on my conscience. I cannot support your request in good faith."* She opened her folder and said, *"I've got a list of programs here which I want you to think about. They'll teach you to do good work with your hands, work you can be proud of. They will provide you with the skills you need to do good work your entire life, and I think this is going to be a better choice."*

I was totally blown away. At first, I was sad because clearly she didn't understand me. I have scars, physical and emotional, all over my body. I have them because I survived and overcame what she kept referring to as my failures. When she looked at me and considered my experiences, all she saw was, *"You fail a lot"*, not *"Wow, you overcame a lot!"* or, *"Wow, you climbed out of a lot of holes."* Just, *"You failed a lot."*

It made me sad. Then I became angry. I looked around her office again at all those plaques, all those awards. I tried to imagine how many young people walked through her door with dreams so big they could barely contain them. Did she manage to get each of them to accept something that was more easily digested, something that could fit in their pockets that she could show to people and be proud of? I wondered if this was how she treated all her special kids, or if it was just me. Either way, it was clear that my champion had taken it upon herself to edit my dream. I had enough, I didn't need one more "agent of reality."

I watched the tears run down her face. After a long silence, I thanked her for her time, stood, and walked out of her office. I never turned around. I never went back. I never followed up. I never asked for the dollars they were legally obliged to provide me for audio textbooks and computer software. I never asked for their support again. I told myself, "I don't want any of it. If I'm going to do this, clearly, I will have to do it alone." It wouldn't be the first time. I thought this time, with the support I needed, things would be different and easier. I was wrong. Luckily, my mama had given me everything I needed. *Inevitable Victory for*

Hasan. With love, Mom. I knew it was on me to figure this out because I had to go face my Upward Bound students in nine months, and I had to reassure them and myself that we deserved an opportunity to achieve our dreams.

The Hard Way It Is

Realizing that I wasn't going to receive the support I needed from vocational rehab, or the law school, I knew that this journey would possibly be as challenging as Berea. With Dreama supporting me, and new friends who I believed would become allies, I was determined to make UK Law work. I knew I would have to get myself involved in as many activities and organizations as I could. I ran for, and was elected, President of the First Year Law Class.

Dreama was a tremendous resource, especially with helping me process and understand the materials at a depth I could not achieve just by trying to read the books. However, I still struggled to maintain my grades. I hated law school, but I refused to quit. I loved many of the students and faculty I had met, but there were some who clearly felt I did not belong.

My case law textbooks were huge. For a person with dyslexia and ADHD, law school can easily be an intimidating and challenging experience, and it can be difficult to find success. I relied heavily on building good relationships with peers and professors as I had in the past, but realized I was not going to be able to find success reading all the required case law books. Professors generally frowned on students using Outlines and Canned Briefs (like Cliff Notes for law cases). In fact, many announced on the first day of class that they were not acceptable tools even though just about every law student I have ever known has a set for each class.

I realized the most important first step for me was to get the basics. I was confident I could gain the rest through engagement with my friends and classmates. Maybe it was the fact that I carried my outlines and briefs openly and used them openly in class to keep up with the professors as they lectured that this became an issue. I was reminded more than a few times that my professors did not think those tools appropriate in a law school classroom. What I heard was, *"People who cannot do this work the way normal people do should not be in my class, in my profession, in my presence."* As a self-advocate, I refused to cower to the pressure of trying to make others feel comfortable with my differences; not anymore, never again.

Instead, I would remind myself that I wasn't here on scholarship, and I had worked hard to make it to UK Law. I was going to do what I was required to do to succeed in the absence of a better support system. This was about me. It was about my students back at Upward Bound and me. Unfortunately, my carrying those learning tools with me into every classroom did not go over well. That wasn't my concern and I decided to let it go.

As the first year progressed, I found myself deeply involved in the law school experience. As the First Year Law Students' Class President, I was involved in the selection committee for the new Dean of the school. I also had great social success and built a peer network I hoped would help bolster my academics, but I was struggling. I hadn't yet built a strong enough relationship with my new friends in which I felt comfortable sharing my challenges.

I requested that the law school allow me some accommodations for the first semester finals. I asked to use a computer to type my exam. There were concerns about storing answers on the computer and because it would not be handwritten, it would no longer be anonymous. I suggested that I could use a word processor to type it and they could have someone transcribe the typed pages into the blue testing books. Although they rejected providing a word processor, a transcriber, or a computer (these would all be considered to set a precedent for future requestors), I did convince the law school to at least allow me to bring and use my own computer. So, I had to haul my desktop Mac computer across campus to each exam, print the exam in the library, and turn it in with all of the other handwritten finals in the provided blue testing books.

At the end of the fall semester, all I wanted to do was go see my mother. I needed to surround myself with people who believed in me and loved me unconditionally. I needed to recharge.

Upsetting the Status Quo

I purchased a Greyhound Bus ticket home. While waiting for the bus, I was accosted by a half-dozen police officers. It was only my ability to remember the lessons Jikki taught me as a child about how much more important it was for a young black man to survive encounters with wrong-minded cops than to be eulogized as righteous that saved me. I stood there hiding my anger and rage at the interrogation I received just feet away from white passengers who were also bundled up in the cold, waiting for the bus. The irony was not lost on me about how quickly I went from the hallowed halls of justice at UK Law back to being a usual suspect.

When I returned to school after the break, I learned I received a couple of low marks on my final grades and would be returning on academic probation. It was more difficult to figure out how to be successful and find allies in a highly competitive environment like law school where everyone looks to be top student.

In my second semester, I began experiencing subtle resistance to my presence at UK Law. One professor chose to completely ignore me in his class, going as far as to skip right over me in conversations, even though we all knew he had a distinct pattern to his classroom engagement. Whether he was going left to right by row or front to back, I was the only student he would not call on when it was clear that I would be in the hot seat next. My classmates asked me how I got to be so lucky, or joked I must have some dirt on the professor to make him not call on me. I knew the answer was much less comical.

Another professor decided to call me out in a class one day. I admit I didn't have a textbook for the class. Besides my outline of the subject, I had not studied the particulars of the case we were reviewing that day. When the professor called on me, I had no problem saying, *"I'm sorry, Professor. I did not complete the reading last night and am not prepared to review this case today. If you call on me tomorrow, it'll give me time to prepare."* (In my mind, this request was a simple accommodation, but once my friends and classmates close by let out an audible gasp, I remembered this was law school. There was no such thing as a simple accommodation.)

"Mr. Davis, I'm sure you can figure it out," he said. My friends began sliding highlighted textbooks and notations in front of me, hoping to give me a chance to not completely embarrass myself. However, I decided if he wanted me to figure it out, then I should oblige him. I proceeded to tell an amazing story of injustice and wrongdoing that left the protagonist maligned and seeking justice.

It was a great story. About two minutes into my creative interpretation of the case law combined with Grimm's Fairytales, the professor interrupted my review of the facts and calmly asked, *"Mr. Davis, do you mind if I ask someone else to help you?"* I calmly responded, *"No, I don't mind, I think that would be fine."* Even though I made it a point to be better prepared in the future, I was not called on again. I decided I would never be shamed or embarrassed in a classroom again.

Finding Allies

These negative experiences were offset by the presence of some really wonderful and supportive professors. Bob Lawson, John Batt, and Bill Fortune were some of my early advocates and supporters. Eventually, Professors Carolyn Bratt and Roberta Harding and Adjunct Professor Allison Conlely joined my team of champions. They taught and interacted with students in ways that made me want to be in their presence and learn what they had to teach.

As a whole, law school was not a very flexible learning environment for someone like me. I stayed engaged and worked as best I could, relying on friends and classmates for support. Although second semester was very difficult, I made it to the end of the first year and completed my exams.

The school's legal career department thought that, as an African American man who volunteered to argue his case twice in the Legal

Writing Seminar (one of my classmates quit, leaving someone without a partner) and a great communicator, I would be a very high draw for a summer law internship. My skills as an actor and storyteller made me quite comfortable in the courtroom. They thought I would be popular with the downtown law firms.

However, I refused to create a resume and interview for summer law internships. I heard great stories of golf outings with partners and late lunches at the country club. I heard students bragging about earning as much as $3,000 a week at some of the most prestigious law firms. I wanted none of it, mostly because I was afraid I would like it, a lot. I thought that to experience luxury like that without earning it, especially after my experiences, would make it hard not to get overwhelmed by the experience and forget why I was in law school. I also didn't want to end up as some employer or law firm's token diversity piece.

I heard stories from upperclassmen who were wined and dined and treated very well every summer, but when they graduated and expected a lucrative offer from the firms that had previously fought over them for three years, too often, an offer never came. Besides, I already had summer work. It would be for 1/3 the pay and three times the work, but I still had work to do and promises to keep. I had been accepted to return as staff in the Berea College Upward Bound. I put all of my law school worries behind me and started preparing for my summer there.

CHAPTER THIRTEEN

THESE ARE MY PEOPLE

"The only child we cannot reach is the child we refuse to touch."
Hasan Davis, J.D.

All In

The summer of 1993, I became the Director of Activities for the Berea College Upward Bound program. I was excited to be back with my students even though I was paid $1300 for six weeks of work being on call 24 hours a day for six days a week. These were my people, the ones few others chose to believe in, and I could not let them down. I had to go back to make sure that, as more of my students were getting closer to graduating high school, they were prepared and encouraged. If there were conversations about falling down to be had, whether theirs or mine, part of a conversation would be about how we get up gracefully.

As I continued with my own academic struggles, I kept going back to my kids to say, "Look where I am now. Mark this spot. I'm going back in." I have received letters over the years from young people telling me how much they appreciated my work. One wrote: "Hasan, you won't believe it. I know I was crazy and I ignored you at first, but because you didn't give up on me, I pushed myself and found success. I've got a family now and I know that's because you showed me, as a role model, that I could be a success as a person and as a father."

Hope Wanted

When the Upward Bound program ended that summer, I was invited to co-lead a Wilderness Adventure Camp (WAC). I had heard of wilderness adventure camps in which the staff hikes a group of kids up into the mountains and they survive off the land. This experience would be unique for me as well as the youngsters since we were creating a unique camping experience for kids who lived in a group home or were heavily involved with Social Services, as foster kids, or kids who had been abandoned or abused. These kids had social, emotional, and behavioral challenges that prevented them from engaging in what most consider normal summer camp experiences, like attending the 4-H or the conservation camps.

The plan was to take them up into the hills of Casey County. There, we were to help them pitch tents, dig latrines, build fires, cook, explore their surroundings, and do team and self-esteem building

112

activities. It sounded like the kind of work that fired me up, so I agreed to co-lead.

When we started preparing for our weeklong wilderness adventure, I received my first training in Safe Physical Management, which was the basic training for anyone working with kids in a juvenile justice, child welfare, or congregate care setting. It was a combination of Aikido and other methods of restraint that were used when a young person instigated a dramatic episode or behavior outburst, or if they became noncompliant and resistant. The goal was to minimize danger to the kids and the staff. For me, the training complemented the Jujitsu and Kung Fu training that I had received growing up.

One of the things I did to prepare was to visit the group home. I needed to visit with one young person in particular whose social worker was very concerned about his attending the camp. K was 11 years old; the day I met him, he was under close physical management, or one-on-one supervision. I approached what appeared to be a tool shed where a man at the door sat peering into the shed. Moving closer, I heard feet shuffling. Before I reached the shed, a little head of brown hair popped above the windowsill, barely able to see out. I thought to myself, *"So, this is the new coatroom."*

After I introduced myself to the staff member, I said hi to K who was back sitting in the center of the mat on the floor of the shed. I was informed he spent a lot of time out here to prevent him from harming himself. His mother had severely abused him and at that point, he often tried to hurt himself. I instantly took a liking to him. He reminded me a lot of my brother Sean. But I wanted this to end differently.

K had burns and cut scars up and down his arms. I asked if I could come in from the heat and talk to him in his cool room. He invited me in and before I could sit, immediately began to cross-examine me. *"Who are you? Why are you here? Am I in trouble? What are you doing? Why are you talking to me?"* They were all great questions. So, I sat down and talked to him about a camp we were planning where we'd be outside, pitching tents, and hiking through the woods. I asked if he would like to be a part of something like that. He lit up, and said that he would love to be a part of it. *"But,"* he said interrupting his own excitement, *"I don't think they're going to let me do that."*

"Well, how about this," I responded. *"If you want to be a part of it and promise that you will do everything in your power to have a great week and show that you can be trusted in the woods with us, I will do everything I can to help you get to camp."*

He stood and looked into my eyes for the first time. *"I promise."*

"Okay." I said. *"I'll talk to your social worker."* K was beside himself at the possibility that he might be allowed to go. I said, *"So, this is our agreement: You're going to watch your behavior for the next week to make sure that you don't do anything that is going to get you into trouble so you can't go. Then you can come, and when we're there, you will be my partner in success."* K thought it was a great idea. We shook on it, and made a plan to see each other at the Wilderness Adventure Camp.

I talked to his social worker and explained that I thought K would be great at camp. She almost laughed at me. She finally said, *"Well, we'll give it a try if you really want to go there, but I will plan to drive up mid-week to bring him home when you realize that this won't work."* I was disappointed by her lack of faith in him, but it was indicative of the attitude I've encountered from other professionals whose job is suppose to be making sure young people in crisis get to a better place and have better experiences.

What is sad is that eventually some of those professionals lose the ability to believe and hold onto the hope of a better future for these children, and you can't give what you don't have. I firmly believe hope is one of the things you have to have in order to give it; you can't dish it out of an empty pot.

In spite of the social worker's doubts, we prepared to welcome K and the rest of our new young friends to camp. The leadership team packed all the tents and equipment, and then headed to the campgrounds to prepare for our campers.

The volunteers who joined us were a group of professionals who worked with young people in a number of capacities. They included social work students, 4-H extension officers, clinical counselors, and former foster kids. My co-leader was the Director of Activities at the group home. It was a great group, all professional, all with college degrees, some with advanced degrees, who wanted to give these young people, who supposedly didn't have the capacity for this kind of experience, a chance.

The Wildest Adventure

When the kids arrived at Camp WaKonDaHo, we gave them the prepared backpacks full of all the things they needed for the week. None of the kids had to worry about bringing things from the home, only themselves. We packed up all the gear and all started hiking up the Big Hill, about a mile up from the campgrounds. By the time we arrived at our site, there was a lot of complaining and groaning; these kids didn't get outdoors much and had few opportunities do so.

A big part of our experience was introducing the kids to nature through nature walks, art projects, and talks about safety. The only ones with flashlights were the adults, and soon it got very dark. Many of these kids were not country kids, so the fact that they had no lights kept them close to camp.

K was becoming an amazing partner in success. He did have a few outbursts, but so did a number of other kids. These were kids facing challenges. Our job was to show them that with the right tools and/or support, they could get past these little challenges and stay connected to the group. I remember one day, one of the campers had a traumatic episode – a flashback. He had previously been abused, and even though he was having this great experience at camp, something triggered him. He crawled into his tent screaming; reflexively one of the staff members tried to crawl in to calm him, which completely set him off. A large man crawling into a small place with a kid who has experienced severe trauma, the extent of which we could only guess, is not so effective. So, we regrouped and tried to put all of our professional heads together and come up with a Plan B, but none of the adults had an answer. We noticed the other kids were starting to get agitated.

As K returned to camp with the firewood collection team, he saw the commotion and immediately ran to his tent. We stopped and told him to step back because we were trying to solve a problem. After all, if there is a problem to solve, then it must be an adult's responsibility to solve it. However, K quickly became agitated too because his tent mate was in pain and he wanted to be part of the solution. Recognizing this, and realizing that eventually this was going to turn into something we would have to manage with K too, I called him over. I kept it simple saying, *"K, your tent mate is having a hard day, and we don't know how to get him back on track. What would you suggest?"*

K sat and thought with me for a minute, and then he said, *"Can I go in and talk to him?"* A couple of the adults thought this would be a bad idea, and we definitely should not allow it. We were in a situation where all the things that normally worked weren't working.

I tell folks all the time that once you've exhausted all of the obvious answers, you have to go outside the box and look for something you believe makes no sense at all; this was one of those times. I replied, *"All right, K, see what you can do."*

K slowly crawled inside and made his way to the back part of the tent where his tent mate was rolled into a ball. He just sat there with him, and after a few minutes we overhead him say, *"You know, this has been a great week, and part of the reason is because you are here. If you have to leave, I don't think it is going to be as good, so we need you to come out and be with us now."* That was it. He said his piece and sat with his friend.

After a minute, his tent mate stretched out, took a deep breath, wiped his eyes, and said, *"OK."* Then they crawled out of the tent together.

It was an amazing moment for K. For the first time, perhaps ever, he didn't see himself as the problem; he was part of the solution. He realized he could be useful and valuable, and I found that amazing.

The first few days were going pretty well. I carried the only actual weapon on the hill, a big military-issue combat knife which we used it to hack down weeds and cut twine for lashing, a skill the kids got very good at. They were very inventive, so when faced with squatting over a hole all week to use the bathroom, they lashed together two tree limbs between other trees so that we had a comfortable perch. It reminded me of Swiss Family Robinson!

On day three, while the adults were planning the next activity, K asked if I would cut some twine for him. I told him I was talking and would help him in just a minute, but he was very emphatic and excited; it had to be now. After the third time he asked, I pulled my knife out, turned it around, and handed it to him handle first, just like I had explained to him on the first day about how to safely handle a knife. I then returned to my conversation. The other adults were standing still, frozen with their gaze fixed just past me. I took the cue and slowly turned to see K behind me. He held the knife in his hand and stared at me as dumfounded as the adults. I thought about my safe physical management and all the other skills that I had honed as a martial arts student and soldier. I hoped that this wasn't one of those moments where my decision would hurt a child. First, I decided I would try some of my more subtle skills: mediation training, and de-escalation techniques--the really good stuff.

"What's up, K?"

He looked at me and asked, *"Do you know that you just handed me a big old knife and turned your back on me?"*

"Yeah, K, I know. Is that a problem?"

He looked at me, then at the knife, then back at me, as if pondering my question, then smiling, he said in a casual tone, *"No, no it's not."*

I continued watching as he turned around and went to cut the twine for lashing. When he finished, he came back, turned the knife around handle first, and handed it to me. He said, *"Thank you,"* and hopped off to lash together pieces of wood with the twine he had cut.

Later that day, we were in the middle of a group project when, without warning, but as promised, K's social worker arrived. As soon as K saw her hiking up the hill, he spiraled. He began screaming, cursing, and punching trees. As if on cue, she smiled and said, *"It looks like I got here just in time."* I was angry and frustrated. We talked with her a while and convinced her to stick around hoping we could show her the real Camper K before she tried to drag him from this mountain. Just then, another counselor called out K's name as K bolted into the woods, something the social worker took as an affirmation of everything she believed about him. It was getting close to dark, and we were preparing for dinner.

We asked the other staff to continue preparations for dinner with the campers, and asked the social worker to join us for our evening meal. Then, as the sun began to fade, I started down the path after K. I walked for about twenty minutes. It was dark now, and ahead of me, I could hear heavy breathing. I called out to K, and he called back. *"Are you okay?"* I asked, moving towards the heavy breathing. He said he was, so I continued walking at my pace until I finally caught up with him sitting on a log.

I sat down on the log with him and turned off my flashlight. We just sat a while, and then I asked him what his biggest fear was. He answered it was that his social worker was coming to take him back to the shed at the group home. He was afraid they were going to lock him in that box and never let him out again. I told him I would do everything I could to keep that from happening, but he needed to do his part to keep them from thinking he deserved to be in a box. *"It is hard for me to explain to her how great your week has been if as soon as she shows up, you turn back into that person she thinks you are."*

Once K was settled, we decided to head back to camp. We walked and talked about how to respond if he did have to leave and what he could take away from this experience that still made it useful, especially the new ways of looking at his old problems. We went through a couple of different scenarios about how to figure out where he was, how he got there, and how to turn it into something useful.

When we got back, the social worker was beside herself. The other students had gathered the firewood and put together a grand campfire feast. They did all the things that needed to be done. After dinner, a number of us talked with her and explained that K was having an exceptional week. Aside from her arrival, it seemed like he was on track to be a great camper. It took a bit of work, but we finally convinced her she should leave him with us. He had already been there three days, so there wasn't time for much more to happen. She finally agreed to let him stay.

We finished the week strong. At our closing ceremony, we gave all the students paper plate awards and allowed them to give awards to each other too. It was a very empowering opportunity for them to speak about the help they had received throughout the week as they were able to recognize those kids and adults who had championed them. It was an opportunity to have their hard work and effort reflected back to them. I felt it had been a great week and I think all our staff felt the same. We had taken this opportunity to create something unique for kids, the ones who no one even trusted to walk down the hall alone. We all hoped that it might be something that sparked more opportunities.

At our closing fire, we asked everyone to write down several things they wanted to eliminate from their lives on a piece of paper. Then as part of our ceremony, we allowed them to burn the papers and speak about their lives without the burdens they carried. It was a powerful moment to see and hear young people speak so clearly and eloquently about their experiences and challenges, while talking so positively about their paths from this point forward.

K returned to the group home a different young man. Over the next year, I heard he reenrolled in local school, tried out and made the middle school baseball team, and was having more good days than bad. No one can correct these things all at once, but I think the outdoor experience, the opportunity to be out of the home, to be trusted and to gain confidence, allowed him to carry some of that back with him and to let go of the angry frightened boy the world told him he had to be.

CHAPTER FOURTEEN

I'VE HEARD THIS SONG

"Education is not the exclusive providence of those who do not have a diagnosis." Hasan Davis, J.D.

Continuing the Fight

I returned to my apartment in Lexington at the end of the Wilderness Adventure Camp to find a summer's worth of mail waiting for me. One of the letters was from the law school, a notification that I had been expelled for academics. Since I lived across the street, I decided to walk over and figure out exactly what that meant. My final grades put me just shy of the marks I needed to stay in school. In spite of my hard work, I was not able to achieve my optimal result without accommodations or meaningful support.

I was disappointed the law school made the grand gesture of inviting me to be a student, but did not seem very interested in helping me find success. I raised many of these points in my "request for re-admission" letter that I submitted to the Dean. I learned that the re-admission committee did not actually meet again until after the new academic semester began, so I was in a bind. I had volunteered to be a member of the new student orientation team for the incoming class of first year students, so I went about my business preparing for the new school year and planning orientation, all the while waiting to hear if I was actually going to be allowed to return to classes.

As word got around to my classmates, many surprised me with their support. Some even offered to strike if I did not get readmitted. If you know anything about the typical law student, you know this was an incredible gesture. On the other hand, the Dean and some other students kept reminding me that I wasn't a law student anymore, and perhaps shouldn't be involved in new student orientation. But, I had made a commitment and as the first year class president, I felt it my duty to carry out my promise. Until the committee confirmed that I wasn't a student anymore, I intended to continue business as usual.

Finally, a decision was made to readmit me on probation. The Dean explained that as an additional condition of my probation, I would be required to attend special courses and remediation. She further directed that I would not be allowed to seek or hold any student government leadership positions while on probation. All my classmates knew I intended to remain involved in student government, and I was already putting together a slate to run for President of the UK Law School Student Government Association.

Sadly, what she did not mention was any desire from the law school to learn more about my learning needs. She didn't ask for any strategies that might be implemented to support my successes. No one offered to act as a liaison, to develop strategies for educating my professors about my needs in order to ensure I was not marginalized or isolated because I would have to study, prepare, and test differently than other students. So, I was frustrated by the assumption the law school made, deciding what was best for me and scripting my expected course of action without any input from me or dialogue about how the law school could best work with me to minimize the impact of my disability. I did not consider myself lucky because they decided to let me stay. I considered myself more determined to have the same kind of experiences as my peers.

When the Dean finished laying down the rules I would have to abide by, I asked her if these policies were the standard policies put in place for every student who was on probation. (I later learned there were quite a few students on probation each semester.) *"No, these are just for you."* I told her that I would probably not abide by them if all the other students on probation were not held to the same restrictions. I didn't think it was fair. I thanked the Dean for her support in returning to law school, and then returned to planning my upcoming campaign for president.

My slate of officers did very well and sent the close election to a recount. It was conducted very quickly with no observers, and I was simply told that we lost by one of the narrowest margins in law school history. I did have questions about the result, but I could hear Dreama whispering in my head, *"Things like this happen. You can't win them all."*

Overall, my third semester of law school was going well for me. I had Dreama's support, even though she was now practicing law in Bowling Green, and I was on track in most of my classes. I played intermural sports with some of my classmates and participated in the law school tradition of attending the Fall Meet at Keenland Racetrack.

Not Invisible

I also met one of my greatest classroom challenges in my second year. I had a required class with a professor who seemed to make a point of ignoring me for the entire semester. Everyone recognized and commented on the odd exchanges, or lack of exchanges, in the classroom. I was determined that I would not be made invisible again. Although he never called on me, I worked very hard to be prepared for his class and interjected my thoughts and analysis whenever I could. Even then, he seemed to move away from my remarks and would quickly engage other students.

One day the professor was late to class. The other students began whispering about the "fifteen minute professional courtesy rule." I had never heard of it, but it intrigued me. My classmates excitedly explained that if a professor is late to class by fifteen minutes, the students were no longer obligated to remain and could not be marked as absent for the period. *"Wow,"* I thought, *"where was this rule all my life?"* So, as the long hand slowly ticked itself toward the three, my friends began packing books and preparing for the mass exodus. At exactly fifteen minutes past the hour, the entire class rose to its feet. At exactly fifteen minutes and five seconds past the hour, the door to our classroom opened and in walked our professor.

All my classmates immediately took their seats leaving me alone, standing and pushing past the chairs of friends towards the exit. I could feel the eyes of entire class following me as I reached the end of my row and headed down the lecture hall stairs. The professor watched me a moment more, then asked what I was doing. As I turned to explained my new nugget of higher education wisdom -- the fifteen minute rule -- I could see many of my friends and classmates slowly shaking their head trying to discourage what they all saw coming.

After months of being ignored and treated by him as if I were invisible, I was done being demeaned by another person intent on humiliating me. I could no longer allow him to choose when he would acknowledge my very presence. After listening to my explanation, he acknowledged the practice, smiled and reminded me that he was now in the classroom, and suggested I quickly take my seat.

But it was too late; after all the days I felt he had gone out of his way to make me invisible and powerless in this class, I was not going to be disappeared again. Glancing around the room, I took a deep breath as I considered his request. I returned his smile as I opened the door and said, *"I look forward to seeing you tomorrow."*

CHAPTER FIFTEEN

LIFE INTERRUPTED

"If you keep doing what you have always done, your competition will get better and you will get worse results." John Maxwell

"Go Time"

The phone rang about 3:00 a.m., and I woke up agitated. In my experience, nobody has ever gotten a "You won the lottery!" call at 3:00 a.m., but I *have* had a great deal of bad news come at this hour. I snatched up the phone.

"Hello?"

"I'm in some real shit, Hasan."

I knew it was serious as soon as I recognized Derrick's voice. I hadn't spoken to Derrick or Sean much in the last year, not since I started law school. The further into school I got, the more they drew back. I don't know if they were trying to protect me or trying to avoid being subjected to disappointment, whether mine or theirs. So, for him to call me meant he was in big trouble and there was nobody else to call.

It was very bad. He started to speak again, and I interrupted him, *"You know if you say anything, I probably won't be able to help you."* At this point, I could only imagine I was about to walk a very thin line between advisor and accomplice. I didn't want to get caught up in what was happening with him, not this close to my goal.

Derrick refocused, took a breath, and said, *"I need help."* I looked for a pencil and some paper, and I started down my checklist - the usual questions.

"Are you hurt?"

"No."

"Are your girl and the baby okay?"

"They're fine."

"You have a number I can reach you at?"

"Yes."

"Are you safe?"

It took him a while to answer that one.

"For now."

My head started racing through all the crazy possibilities - from drug deals gone wrong to gang turf wars. No matter how I thought about it, it was a bad situation.

"Where are you now?"

"I am at a little hotel."

"What city?"

"Near Tampa."

I told him it was going to take me a bit to get something worked out, but I would. Before I hung up, I told him, *"Just keep your head down."*

I realized my body was humming, shaking from the adrenalin. I was frustrated, afraid, angry, and disappointed. I don't know if the disappointment was with my brothers or me. The last time I got a call like this was back at Berea when Sean called about Derrick getting shot. After I got through that one, I promised myself I was never going to get pulled into somebody else's drama again.

I thought I was good, that I was over it, that I didn't have to be responsible for them anymore, and then I reached into the back of my closet and pulled out my go bag. It was the same emergency bag I have had in one form or another since I was a teenager. It was packed with all the things that I needed to quickly disappear. I didn't have a lot of time to think, but I knew I had to make another call. I picked up the phone and dialed. She answered on the first ring. It caught me by surprise,

"What's wrong?" she said.

Dreama and I had been together long enough to understand my behavior.

"It's Derrick."

"What happened?"

"I think he's in trouble, and I have to find a way to get to him."

"What kind of trouble?"

"I didn't ask."

I was waiting for the cross-examination. When you've got a mind even half as sharp as Dreama's, questions come quick and the expectation for answers comes right after. We had been at this place before, through all the other madness. I figured she'd start asking me about my decision. I expected to hear statements and questions like: *"You said it wasn't going to happen again. You are going to mess up everything you've been working for. What about your life? What about our life?"*

I was trying to figure out where she was going to start so I could have the right answer and come up with some sort of response. Instead, she just said, *"Okay. Be safe. Call me when you figure it out."* Then she hung up. I wasn't sure if she meant *"See you later," "Good luck,"* or *"Don't call me again."* I did not have time to think about it. Clearly, I was going to have another conversation with her; at least I hoped I would. I rolled over and tried to go back to sleep. In a few hours, the sun would rise, and I would work out how to get to Tampa. The clock was running.

The first thing I did the next morning was to call Mr. Edwards who owned a local car rental business. Unlike the national rental car chains, Mr. Edwards didn't require a credit card, but he did require cash upfront and a big deposit. He was reasonable, all things considered. I walked over to the bank, where I still had a couple thousand dollars of student loan money left for the semester to cover rent and bills through the holidays. I had been hoping I could use some of that money to get a used car; it would have been my first vehicle, but I guess it wasn't the time.

At the bank, the clerk told me I had to talk to a manager. I needed to be counseled on my decision to withdraw so much of my money at that time because it would put me close to the minimum balance. I was focused on what I needed to do, and I didn't pay a lot of attention to the fact that it was an obviously slanted conversation. I explained I needed to take care of a family emergency and needed to get there as quickly as I could. I am sure they were imagining all the illegal ways I planned on spending my education dollars; they had no clue. I thanked them all for their assistance,

When I arrived at Mr. Edward's, it was already late afternoon; the winter sun was starting to set as it crossed the sky. We talked a bit and negotiated what a two-day rental might look like, including 1,500 free miles. I laid out a row of hundred dollar bills and took my hand written receipt. I studied the contract and the substantial additional charge for every mile over 1,500 and every day past two. I threw my emergency bag in the car, checked the gauges, and started chasing the sun west to highway I-75 South. If things went well, I figured I'd make Atlanta by midnight. If I could avoid the speed traps, I might be in Tampa by sunrise.

When I arrived outside of Tampa, I sat at the phone booth waiting for a response from the pager number Derrick gave me. A few minutes later, the out-of-tune chime shook the booth. Derrick sounded like he hadn't slept since we talked yesterday morning. I jotted down some directions and a couple of landmarks, did the math in my head, and told him I needed about thirty minutes. He and Heather needed to be ready to roll. As I started to hang up, he added, *"Hasan, I got another girl here too."*

"What?"

"I got another girl, and we can't leave her here."

I took a deep breath and thought about the time we were killing. It had been more than twenty-four hours already. Our window of opportunity was closing fast.

"Alright, man, I will be there in less than thirty minutes, then we gotta roll."

131

I stopped at the gas station a few exits before the meeting spot, filled the tank, and bought bags of snacks and drinks. I figured we could get close to Atlanta before we needed to refuel again.

I pulled off the highway into a nearly deserted motel parking lot. I saw a door open at the end of the row of rooms, drove over, popped the trunk and unlocked the doors. Two girls exited the room. I recognized Heather. She was carrying my new niece, Amber, wrapped in a blanket.

Derrick quickly introduced the other woman as Angel - just Angel. She climbed into the back seat on the driver's side without speaking. Derrick looked at me. He looked bad, worse than I had seen him in a long time, and I had seen him look pretty bad. We hugged quickly, but we didn't say anything.

Sometimes It Is As Bad As It Seems

I grabbed the last of the bags, tossed them into the trunk, and closed the door to the motel room. Once on the highway, the radio did most of the talking. That silence only lasted about an hour until we passed our first State Trooper. I could sense everybody in the car get tense. That was when I realized I was doing something different from what I originally imagined.

Until now, I assumed he was outrunning thugs, gangs, or pimps, but now, it was obvious that they were afraid of the law. Derrick saw the look on my face, and his expression turned to one of sadness. I don't know if he was sad because he had dragged me back into his craziness or sad because I had no idea what I was getting myself into. It didn't matter either way.

After that first incident, I was anxious every time we passed a police car, an ambulance, a tow truck; anything that had flashing lights got my attention. It is hard to be inconspicuous driving down the road looking as exhausted and stressed as we looked. I tried to drive slowly and calmly. Finally, exhaustion replaced the adrenalin they had been running on for the last few days and they all fell asleep. It was just me alone in the car listening to some oldies music station and the occasional whimper from Baby Amber talking me into the sunset.

On our way through Atlanta, we dropped Angel, Heather, and Amber off with family. I returned to Kentucky with Derrick. When we got to my apartment, Derrick explained the whole ordeal. I began to piece together our next move. I had been preparing myself for tough news, but I was still not ready for the truth. He told me the story of an enraged driver who followed him and his family from the Christmas shopping chaos of a shopping mall parking lot across town to their secluded apartment, how he tried to lose the man several times but was recklessly followed for miles, then finally had to confront the driver filled with road rage in hopes of putting an end to the stalker and protect his newborn baby.

I was crying before he even formed the words. *"He went for his gun, Hasan; I had to choose, so I chose him. I killed a man to protect my baby."* He was crying now. *"I see his face every time I close my eyes."* I sat still, my mind racing over the words, the details, and the defense. I tried to get my thoughts around any way this was not as bad as it sounded. I believe Derrick killed a man in self-defense trying to protect his family. However, every time I played the tape in my head, I imagined the headlines as a local manhunt went national. *Black man wanted for gangland execution, details at eleven.*

CHAPTER SIXTEEN

BACK ON TRACK

"It's So Hard To Say Goodbye To Yesterday" (Lyrics)

Boyz II Men

No Turning Back

After Derrick's confession, I returned to school still struggling to get my head back into classes. At the same time, I tried to figure out how I could get my brother turned over to the law, alive. I committed to giving it my undivided attention as soon as finals were over. After all the hard work I had put into turning classes around, I was determined not to let it all slip away. Using assistive technology, especially a personal computer, was still new territory on college campuses, and unheard of in the culture of UK Law School.

During my third semester of finals, I hauled my Mac desktop computer over to the law school for each final and set it up in one of the student study lounges. On the morning of my Constitutional Law II final, I joined my classmates in the classroom before the exam and began, like everyone else, to review my outlines and notes. It was the same routine which takes place before every final in every law school in the country, with nervous students all trying to glean the last bit of useful information, hoping to hold on to it long enough to get it all on the page. The professor began to pass out the Blue Books students use to write their exam answers. All the students wrote their unique identification numbers on the book. This was supposed to ensure each test would be graded without any knowledge of which student had written it. Of course, it is hard to remain anonymous when yours is the only exam which has been typed and printed from a computer.

As students continued to cram, the professor walked over to me and voluntarily acknowledged me for the first time, asking what I was looking at. I told him it was my outline as I looked around at all the other students still doing the same. He stepped a little closer, then said, *"Mr. Davis, you do realize that you can't use the outline during the test, right?"*

Maybe if I had not been distracted by all of the other things going on in my life, I would have been able to process his words differently. However, those words crawled all over me. I stood up to voice my opinion, maybe even express that I had finally had enough of his subtle attempts to make me feel that I was not good enough for his law school. Fortunately, my friend Bill was sitting behind me. He put his hand on my shoulder, and he gave me the look that said, *"Don't give him what he wants; don't make him right."* I sat down and returned to my outline, without acknowledging the professor.

The situation set me in a tailspin right before the exam. I very publicly and loudly stacked all of my outlines and notes on the desk before I left the classroom for the lounge. Even typing my answers, I couldn't stop thinking about the encounter in the classroom. When I finished typing the exam answers, I copied the file to a floppy disc, went to the library, printed a copy, and returned to the classroom to turn it in. I was done. I could not wait to get out of that building.

The Same Old Drama

During the holiday break, Derrick and I spent most of our time trying to figure out how to safely turn him in to the authorities and I spent a lot of time studying my Criminal Law textbooks – probably more than I had for the class itself. Over Christmas, I decided to take him with me to Bowling Green. We spent a few days with Dreama who was still in the dark about the details of Derrick's situation.

When I got back to Lexington, I went to the law school to check my grades and discovered I had not received a grade in the Constitutional Law II class. Instead, I had received an "E." When I inquired at the office what that meant, they said it meant I didn't turn in a test for that class. This meant I failed, and I would receive another letter shortly. I spoke with several administrators explaining that since I typed my answers, it should have been very easy for someone to notify me if there was a concern. I could have sent another copy to the professor in a timely manner. I was curious to know why nobody thought about contacting me. Certainly, this missing (typewritten) paper would have been noticed immediately. Apparently, that didn't seem to cross anybody's mind.

Finally, after a couple of days of talking, they agreed the professor would accept another copy of my exam and grade it. I turned it in again, received a passing grade, and was reinstated as a student for the spring term, but still on probation. It was becoming clear to me that there were some people in the UK Law School who did not want me there. I was not planning to leave without the degree I came to earn.

After ringing in the New Year with Dreama in Bowling Green, I borrowed her car for a week to return to UK Law and get prepared for spring classes. I was still trying to come up with a plan for Derrick and looking for a bona fide self-defense plea; I felt we might have some luck with such a defense. When classes resumed, I made plans to meet with Professor Bob Lawson, hoping he was willing to walk me through a hypothetical scenario that was even more apt to work. Professor Lawson, in addition to being a fellow Berea College graduate and one of the most down to earth and approachable professors I have ever studied under, was and is without question, the foremost expert in the state on Criminal Defense. He actually wrote the Criminal Code for Kentucky.

The Last Ride

Unfortunately, a few days into the spring semester, I received a call from Dreama. She told me she was visited by two FBI agents who wanted to make her aware that her automobile had been spotted in Lexington transporting a passenger of interest in an ongoing investigation. I had not told Dreama what was going on with Derrick beyond the usual "he is going through some hard times" spiel. Although she wanted answers immediately, I was not prepared to give her any more than that. I promised her that I would explain everything to her when I returned with her car on the weekend.

"We are out of time," I told Derrick. *"They are coming for you."*

Derrick's entire body relaxed. *"Good,"* he said, *"I can't keep putting you through this. It is time to handle my business."*

We packed a few of his things and agreed it would be best to take him back to Berea. My friend Keith had returned to Berea before I graduated and had an apartment near campus. After my experience with the Lexington police, I had more confidence in my brother surviving being taken into custody in Berea. It would be hard enough for me to let them take him, so we agreed I should just drop him off and wait for the news.

Like we had done so many times before, we took one last ride to Berea along the back roads I had learned so well since moving to central Kentucky. We drove slowly to make time for talk about all the good times, the crazy bad times, and all the choices we had made for better or worse that brought us to this moment, walking in two different directions; one road was a beginning, the other a dead-end. Derrick apologized again for putting me in harm's way. We talked about his regrets: not joining the army with me and not staying in Kentucky to get into Berea when I returned. We talked about how fear can strangle a person with paralysis.

We arrived in Berea around midnight; Keith was at work, so I let us in. We found some of Keith's holiday hooch left over from New Year's Eve, and had our last drink. *"To brotherhood,"* I said.

"To family," he replied. Then he told me it was time for me to get back to Dreama and my new life. *"The good life,"* he said, and then gave me a hug goodbye. *"Take care of you for me,"* he whispered. *"I'm sorry I won't be there for you."*

I got a call about an hour later that the US Marshalls and the FBI had apprehended Derrick without incident. They charged in with shotguns and assault rifles. Derrick performed just like we rehearsed: he stayed calm, made no sudden moves, didn't talk, and held his hands high with his fingers spread. Like Jikki said, *"The objective is to stay alive."* He did exactly as he was told. He was safely in custody.

Refocused

Once I cleared my head of the last few months of chaos, I focused on getting back on my track to success. During the spring of 1994, I was invited to deliver the National Student Keynote Address at the COOL (Campus Outreach Opportunity League) National Student Service Conference. I joined the Delta Theta Phi International Law Fraternity and was elected president of the Alben W. Barkley Student Senate at UK Law. I also continued to struggle to make the marks academically. Although my requests for accommodations were still mostly challenged, I did find a small cadre of professors who were interested in my success and provided unofficial support.

As expected, Derrick was extradited to Florida to stand trial. The lead prosecutor in the case contacted me and told me that I was being charged with Accessory to Murder. He seemed a little surprised by my calm demeanor as I explained to him my take on his case against me. After we talked for about an hour, he admitted he was trying to scare me so I would cooperate, but since I just corroborated much of what his investigator was telling him, he believed I was "above board." I agreed to meet with the prosecutor's investigator and informed the prosecutor that I would be seeking legal representation before we moved further.

A professor once shared with our class the old adage "An attorney who represents himself has a fool for a client." Well, I wasn't an attorney yet, and definitely did not want to be a fool. Derrick's trial was set for the fall of 1994. I immediately contacted his Attorney and offered myself as his full time assistant on this case, willing to do anything and everything short of actually trying the case, only because I had not graduated from law school yet. His attorney did not allow me to assist.

Stop Playing Small

I returned to my studies with new energy. During spring finals, I was allowed to use my computer, but was warned that I had no formal documentation for accommodations. Funny, I had only been telling the law school that for two years now. With finals complete, I was prepared to get back to my real work, Upward Bound. But first I joined Delta Theta Phi Law Fraternity chapter (Senate) presidents from across the country for the International Delta Theta PHI biannual meeting. There I was elected by my peers across the country to serve as the one of two international student representatives on the DTP Supreme Senate. It was a great affirmation of my presence in the legal world. Now I was ready to get back to my young charges at Berea.

Most of my students from my years as a tutor counselor in the program had already graduated high school. Many had gone on to college, and a few were now Tutor Counselors in the Upward Bound program. We had a second or third wave of younger siblings from the same families.

I remember promising one young man whose older brother was my student, that when he was old enough to come to Upward Bound, I would be there waiting. It was exciting to welcome him to the program. I was blessed to learn new lessons each summer about courage and persistence and I was honored to share my own struggles and triumphs. After a summer of Upword Bound, I returned for another week of Wilderness Adventure Camp. I felt I was living my purpose and was affirmed in what my life work would become.

Returning home from a summer of good work, I approached my overstuffed mailbox with apprehension and dread. To my delight and surprise, I did not have a "Dear Mr. Davis" letter from the law school. I showered and hurried over to check the grades on the board, just to be sure. Unbeknownst to me, I had received a scholarship for my academic performance. The "Most Improved Scholar Award" was given each year to the student who had increased his or her academic performance and overall grade point average by the greatest margin over the previous year. I didn't know there was such an award or that I even had won it until one of my classmates congratulated me. I thought he was congratulating me on being back in school since up to that point, that had been an iffy thing.

"Yeah, yeah. I made it through another year."

"No, you got the Most Improved Scholar Award!"

"What are you talking about?"

"Your name is on the plaque in the hallway."

"You're kidding me!"

We walked out there, and sure enough, right outside the student government office, my name was on a plaque: Most Improved Scholar Award.

"Huh, that's interesting."

"Well, I got that award last year." Sure enough, his name was there above mine. He then added, *"How did you like that banquet?"*

"What banquet?"

"You know, with the Chief Justice of the Kentucky Supreme Court and the entire Bar Assoc..." He stopped abruptly. *"Oh, maybe they didn't have it this year."*

"Yeah, maybe that's it," I responded, then added, *"So is there money with this award?"*

"Yeah, I think there is."

I went to the Dean's Office. *"Apparently I got some award that I wasn't notified about."* Everyone paused. *"I just want to know if this was a cash scholarship."* After a moment more of silence, I was told that it was and someone directed me to the accounting office. I didn't need the party and they didn't want the publicity, but I definitely needed the monetary help. I deposited the check and prepared for the next round. Even though I had managed to get through the previous semester and secure my name on the wall, I was still on probation and taking on even more challenging classes.

Finish What You Started

During the previous semester, I had been pushing for more clearly defined supports and accommodations so I could really show what I was capable of. The school told me I would have to be retested for my disability at my own expense. So, even though I'd had learning disabilities my whole life, I got retested. When I turned the results and recommendations over to the new Dean of Academic Affairs, he explained he wasn't sure if the law school would be willing to make that many adjustments to accommodate one individual. I thought that was quite a bold statement for a representative to make on behalf of a law school.

I took it upon myself to inform my professors of my standing and my needs. Many provided me extraordinary support to ensure my success. Once again, I had to return to and stand before the entire faculty to request support and approval to continue into my final semester. The process had exhausted me, but I continued to think about all of the students who had walked away from institutions like this believing they were not law school material. I thought about the students whom I rush to be with each summer, who often see people like us getting knocked down, and who rarely know someone who is willing to keep getting up just one more time. I knew that if I got too tired to keep fighting, this system would go right back to "the way things have always been."

I made one last effort to complete what I started. After the Academic Dean reduced the maximum course load that I could register for each semester, my professors worked with me to ensure I was able to produce the quality of work representative of my capacity. The last year of school was very productive for me, an opportunity to put the past behind and truly focus on the present. I started taking many seminars in which I could discuss, debate, and expand on ideas, instead of just looking for the right answer. My focus moved to juvenile law and mental health along with negotiation and mediation. These were skills I believed were very important to my work, but were not necessary to passing the Bar exam. After a lot of thought, I eventually decided that I would not sit for the Bar. There was plenty of great work to be done, and my law school career had prepared me to fight even harder.

Graduation was an incredible event, with many family members from both St. Louis and Atlanta in attendance, just like when I graduated from Berea. I sent Sean an invitation, but he never responded. I had not talked to him since Derrick's trial. Not long after, I received word that Sean had also been arrested and was in jail. Derrick and Sean both ended up serving life sentences, and it was time for me to get on with my life. Although I would have died for them, I could not live for them. My life had become about possibilities, creating opportunities for others like us, other young people struggling with finding success with too few champions able to recognize or realize they were in the presence of greatness.

143

Years later, I was invited back to discuss the law school experience with college students who were considering UK LAW. I was honest about the best and worst of my experiences. I shared with them the challenges of being a student with identified disabilities and receiving no support. I encouraged them, saying, *"If you have disabilities and want to be a UK Law graduate, apply, because now we know it is possible."* After the conversation, the Dean excitedly pulled me to the side and shared with me that the law school now had a full array of support services for students with disabilities. He also told me the law school actually initiates the conversation with all students every year to ensure that they can be identified as early as possible for support in their success at law school.

Yeah, that made me smile.

CHAPTER SEVENTEEN

FINDING GOOD WORK

"Treat a man as he is and he will remain as he is. Treat a man as he can and should be, and he will become as he can and should be." Johann Wolfgang von Goethe

On The Move

In December of 1995, with my law school classes behind me, I immediately applied for a job transporting elementary students participating in the Lexington YMCA after-school program. I needed to ground myself, needed to refocus and figure out, at this stage of my life, what was important to me. I started making plans to continue my work in youth development, but I unsure how to proceed. Three months later, Lorraine called to ask me to consider returning to Horizons as a mid-term replacement middle school teacher.

Dreama had recently returned to Berea, forfeiting her opportunity to make partner in a firm for a chance to get back to work that was more fulfilling. I planned to move back to Berea and finally try to make our relationship work in a more traditional way. However, the chance for me to answer the call from Lorraine was pulling on me. I knew it was only a few months, and after a six-year long distance relationship I hoped ours was strong enough to hold out a little longer without her giving up on me.

By then, my sister Theresa was teaching at Horizons. All of my nieces and nephews also eventually attended the school. My mother still supported Horizons by giving writing workshops and organizing fundraisers. So, despite the fact that I had been expelled, Horizons continued to be a major part of our family story. Lorraine made working at Horizons exciting because she encouraged creativity and innovation. At that time, it was a place where almost everyone I knew, loved, and respected was involved and engaged in building great futures; it never stopped being my home.

When the school year ended, I returned to Berea College and took a job as an Admissions Counselor. I reconnected with Mr. John Cook, who was still Director of Admissions and now, my boss. Advocating for Berea was the easiest job I ever had. I didn't tell Mr. Cook, but I probably would have done it for free. As part of my work, I was also a part-time Assistant Director of the Black Cultural Center; my job was to develop mentoring programs to support student success. I became an intervention expert, working to help young people who faced academic challenges similar to mine. Dreama and I were finally living in the same town and were starting to talk more seriously about a future together.

Meanwhile, Lexington was experiencing an increase in teen violence and police shootings. The Mayor announced a new initiative by the Knight Foundation to develop a Youth Violence Prevention Task Force. Dreama encouraged me to throw my hat in the ring. She thought that my experiences and accomplishments would be a good fit for this kind of work. She was right as usual. Although my work at Berea was special and important to me, Lexington was the perfect opportunity to finally put to use everything I had learned in my studies, my work, and my own experiences. In the fall of 1997, Mayor Pam Miller held a press conference to introduce me as Lexington's first Director of Youth Violence Prevention. My experience and skills helped me bring together Lexington youth with business and community leaders to develop a comprehensive strategy for addressing youth violence in the Lexington area.

Much of my work was based out of the NCCJ office, the National Conference for Christians and Jews, which gave me access to a team of people who were also engaged in building young people's capacity to be self-advocates and champions for justice. I enjoyed the opportunity to lead young people through the Camp Anytown experience, a weeklong exploration of race, gender, religion, class, and sexual orientation, and the opportunity to help them unpack and create the tools they needed for success. For me, professionally, it was the next opportunity to build the capacity of young people who needed support and encouragement to move beyond their current circumstances. It set me on my course of youth advocacy and justice work.

While in Lexington, I was invited to participate in the Pew Civic Entrepreneurship Initiative (PCEI). The Pew Initiative was designed to help midsize cities harness the creative ideas of citizens in order to address community problems. The experience offered me the opportunity to learn from a broad cohort of entrepreneurs and connected me to a network of national leaders who shared with us their knowledge and expertise. Dreama was invited to participate in the second cohort, giving us a chance to again spend time together further aligning professional trajectories with our personal lives. For two years, I led the Youth Violence Prevention Project highlighted by a citywide Stop Youth Violence Summit. In 1999, Dreama and I decided that it was finally time to live in the same city, as different as it would be from our first ten years. We decided to live in the same house and started thinking about a family.

One of my last assignments as Director of Lexington's Youth Violence Prevention Project was speaking at a workshop conference on the prevalence of violence on college campuses; that is where I met the first Commissioner of Kentucky's Department of Juvenile Justice, Ralph Kelly. After he heard me speak, he said he thought my voice and experience should be part of a larger conversation in the state and asked if he could recommended me for appointment to the Governor's Juvenile Justice Advisory Committee (JJAC) which set policies and provided oversight to hold agencies accountable for juvenile justice issues across the state. Shortly afterwards, I was appointed by Governor Patton. I had served on the JJAC for only a few months when the Chair stepped down. Deciding to throw my hat in the ring to be the new Chair was an easy decision.

My campaign speech outlined a belief that we must speak up for the children, ensuring their needs, whether physical, emotional or social, were properly conveyed to legislators, the governor, and the other people who make decisions about their lives. I explained we needed our state systems to work for kids.

Part of my impassioned plea was fueled by the birth of our first son. I was adamant that no matter what challenges he faced growing up, the systems that were supposed to insure his opportunity to thrive would work better for him than they did for me. This felt like the work I had been preparing for all my adult life. I was elected the new Chair of the Advisory Committee, a position I held for the next ten years, even after it was reorganized by legislation and became the JJAB - Juvenile Justice Advisory Board. Working with other State Advisory Groups (SAGs) and our national partner, the Coalition for Juvenile Justice (CJJ), I was able to increase my knowledge of Juvenile Justice issues and learn about the many reform efforts taking place across the nation.

I utilized this long-term opportunity to begin addressing the most pervasive juvenile justice issues:

• Disproportionate minority contact, the over-representation of youth of color at every decision-making point in the justice system, from a police stop to imprisonment;

• The incarceration of kids who had not committed a crime in secure detention centers and long-term treatment facilities;

• The high rates of youth with developmental disabilities and/or mental health challenges who were removed from an educational setting and eventually experience detention and incarceration; and

• The impact poverty has on significantly increasing the likelihood of juvenile justice involvement.

These were the issues that drove me into the field of juvenile justice and education reform. The more involved I became with the JJAC and CJJ, the more opportunities came for me to learn and become a voice for better laws and more effective youth development models for youth in crisis. I started presenting at conferences and speaking to lawmakers around the country.

While I was Chair of the JJAB, the Office of Juvenile Justice and Delinquency Prevention (OJJDP) went through some changes in leadership and organizational structure. OJJDP created a new Federal Advisory Committee on Juvenile Justice (FACJJ) to advise the new Administrator, Congress, and the President, and to inform the field of Juvenile Justice on the most pressing issues facing young people. They provided advice regarding where we should focus our policies and dollars to address these problems. The Governor appointed me to be Kentucky's first representative to the FACJJ. At our inaugural convening, I was elected Vice-Chair of the Federal Advisory Committee.

Around the same time, I was nominated to participate in the prestigious Rockefeller Foundation Next Generation Leadership (NGL) Fellowship. In 2001, I joined the fourth cohort along with one of the most diverse group of young leaders I have ever encountered. The experience afforded me tools and resources that allowed me to grow in confidence and develop a clear picture of the change I wanted to pursue on behalf of young people. I was honored when I was then invited to join the NGL team as program staff and consultant working with the fifth cohort.

Dreama was now developing education access programs to serve a small number of youth in rural Kentucky. Things were going well for us, personally and professionally. But in 2003, we, together with our first son, lost important people in our lives. Jikki passed in March and a few months later Dreama's father Carlos died. They were both men of integrity and losing them so close together rocked our family. They, like our mothers, were unwavering supporters of our desire for a better world for their grandchildren.

In the spring of 2004, Dreama and I prepared to welcome our second son. We decided that he would be an everyday reminder of our fathers so we named him after them. Carrying the names of both of my fathers and Dreama's father too, our second son arrived to meet the world. Soon after his birth, Dreama and I decided it was time to finally make this twenty years of dating a more official commitment. We were married on December 31, 2004 at Berea College, surrounded by a lifetime of loving supporters.

As the boys grew and Dreama continued expanding her work and influence as a rural education champion, I continued my work in Juvenile Justice at the Advisory group level. Then in 2007, our new Governor of Kentucky appointed a Secretary of the Justice and the Public Safety Cabinet. I met Secretary Brown at a Black History month program at the Administrative Office of the Courts. Over my ten years as JJAB Chair, I worked with previous Justice Cabinet officials, all political appointees. Some were great advocates for children, and some were there to make sure the door stayed locked and the "bad kids" didn't get out. I reasoned it was a good idea to know the man who would be selecting the next leadership team for the Department of Juvenile Justice. I hoped I could at least influence who within the agency might be tapped as the next leader.

I continued my work as a consultant, public speaker, and advocate for young people on the local and national level. Then in late September of 2008, I ran into Secretary Brown at a national Gang Awareness Conference. I reintroduced myself and was pleased that he remembered our first meeting. He asked if I would come by his office to see him sometime. I was, at first, a little nervous, wondering if the Governor had new plans for the JJAB.

At home, I told Dreama about this exchange. A few days later, she asked if I had contacted him, which I hadn't (she's great at reminding me about things). When I did call, his administrative assistant informed me the Secretary wanted to meet with me the following week. I wasn't sure what to think of it; it felt a bit like being called to the principal's office.

When we met, it was already mid-October, and he told me he was putting together the final pieces of his leadership team at the Justice Cabinet. That made me happy; I had a list of Juvenile Justice employees I thought would do a great job of continuing the changes we were trying to make in Kentucky. He shared that his areas of impact included the Kentucky State Police, the Department of Corrections, Criminal Justice Training, Juvenile Justice, the State Coroner's Office, and a few other smaller agencies. He then told me he was looking for a Deputy Commissioner of Operations at the Department of Juvenile Justice and that my name was at the top of his list.

Although I had built a reputation as a youth champion, and of course I voted, I had no ties to the new Governor; I had not assumed I was on anyone's radar. I had no political standing and no one owed me a favor. Secretary Brown said it would be a hard sell, but if I was willing to do the job, he was willing to make the case. In my mind, this was an exercise in futility. However, in my life, there is always room for surprises. I agreed to give him a few weeks to see what he could make happen.

Finding Justice

I was appointed Deputy Commissioner of Operations for the Kentucky Department of Juvenile Justice on November 1, 2008. To hear testimony I gave to the Education and Labor Committee of the U.S. Congress, go to: http://0s4.com/r/49KYQJ

On January 1, 2012, I was appointed State Commissioner of Juvenile Justice, with operational, administrative, and fiscal responsibility for the entire juvenile justice system serving 3,000 young people across the Commonwealth of Kentucky. I managed 1,300 employees and a hundred million dollar budget.

In my first year as Commissioner, I set a strategic planning schedule that would last almost six months and bring together staff from every department in the agency, at every level. The purpose was to determine from the people doing the work, what we did well, what we could do better, and what we should stop doing. Staff across the state seemed energized by the idea that they were going to have a real voice in reimagining the Department of Juvenile Justice (DJJ). Additionally, I gathered our treatment experts from across the agency for a two-day facilitated strategic planning session. Most recognized that DJJ had fallen in line with the prevailing "command and control" corrections model of Juvenile Justice, but admitted a desire to not just punish young people who made mistakes, but instead work to make young people more resilient and better able to move forward with their lives after their involvement with DJJ.

After hearing the report from that gathering, I was certain we were on the right course. I wanted to use new language when introducing DJJ to stakeholders and peers from across the nation, *"At Kentucky DJJ, every child will leave our care more whole, not with more holes."* Once we collected and compiled the feedback from hundreds of DJJ employees, it was clear that the majority of the staff at the Department of Juvenile Justice aspired to be more than a corrections system that served children. They wanted to be a child-serving system that only in its worst cases invoked a corrections response.

At the end of the 2012 legislative session, I was named to a newly formed task force to look closer at the juvenile laws and propose changes to those laws that would address many of the concerns that had continued to come piecemeal before the general assembly in recent years. Chief among them were the status offender issue and the overutilization of referrals to courts from schools.

The task force was comprised of representatives from all three branches of government and related private sector representatives. It included the Deputy Chief Justice of the Kentucky Supreme Court, representatives from the lower courts, prosecutors, and public defenders. There was substantial buy-in and participation on the task force by the child service agencies of the Executive Branch, including me from Kentucky Department of Juvenile Justice. The Chairs of both the Kentucky's House and Senate Judicial Subcommittees served as Co-Chairs of the Taskforce.

We began with agencies submitting data reports and providing presentations about operations, cost, and impact of services over the previous few years. But, because most of our agencies collected and maintained data separately, isolated from other agencies that might often be serving the same child or sibling groups and with no uniformity of the software and hardware used to maintain it, we did not have the capacity or expertise to translate the wide range of data into a single understandable information set that could easily be interpreted or analyzed to inform the work of the Task Force moving forward.

Fortunately, near the end of the first year of the task force, the Pew Charitable Trust's Public Safety Performance Project invited several members, including me, to a convening they were putting on. There they showcased several states that had in recent years initiated radical justice reform in their adult corrections' systems. Kentucky was featured for its work in that area; Representative Tilley from our task force was also one of the legislative leaders in that reform effort. During the convening, we shared with Pew our desire to impact our juvenile justice and other youth serving systems in the same way they had helped other states impact adult corrections and were in the process of supporting the State of Georgia do with new juvenile justice legislation. Although the process of vetting new sites seemed to normally take about a year, I think we were convincing in our belief that with the right support and expert analysis, immediately, we could have concrete data points and identify areas of improvement to present to our legislators in just a few months. It would be enough to both convince them to authorize the task force for another year time and to craft and draft extensive legislation for the next General Assembly.

Kentucky had been identified by Pew as a state that was distinguishing itself through its leadership across the three branches of government. The forming of the task force was seen as a committed first step to real reform in the state. Pew's assistance would put us in the perfect position to jump-start our reform. The Co-chairs, Senator Westerfield and Representative Tilley, made a final impassioned request for immediate assistance from Pew, and it agreed to provide us with a team of analysts to help us make our case for reform. I knew that we were about to change the landscape for the children of Kentucky.

Next Level Thinking

Over the next six months, we gathered enough initial data to convince the General Assembly to reauthorize the Task Force. Partnering with Pew and other key agencies meant reviewing how we analyzed and used placement data and what behavior was being dictated by policy and not by the needs of the individual youth we were serving. At DJJ, we had to be forthright with the data about our systems in order to pinpoint places where our actions and our aspirations were incongruent. Young people who committed misdemeanor crimes were being placed in secure out-of-home placements for nearly as long as young people who had committed egregious felony offenses. We recognized we were spending an exorbitant amount of money securing youth in our detention and treatment facilities, but not nearly enough money providing appropriate treatment options that might successfully maintain these young people outside of facilities, in their home communities. The data told us the latter was a cheaper and more effective treatment option.

The processes we had in place were similar to those in many other states and jurisdictions, allowing staff the discretion to arbitrarily revoke probation for minor incidents; there was no consistent measure of when or why a youth might be sanctioned or what specific behavior could cause a youth to be returned to a locked facility. In addition, every time a child came back into the system, the child had to start at the beginning and go through an extensive multistep process to be eligible for another chance for success at home. This meant that sometimes the same youngster could receive the identical intensive long-term services two to three times. We were spending money, money, money, but seeing few positive results.

Over the next year and a half, I continued to gather feedback from staff about the agency they believed we should be. I coupled it with the data that Pew helped us develop the capacity to access, and everything indicated the system we were operating was not the system we wanted. The information, however, did allow us to begin imagining what a different system would look like. That frightened some of the people in the department. To accomplish these changes, staff would have to grow beyond their fears that changing the system and incarcerating fewer young people might mean they would lose their jobs. I believed there was enough work for everyone in this new model, but it would require a dramatic shift in our culture and thinking about our work, more specialized training for our staff, and greater accountability to successfully transition youth out of our care.

I did understand the possible labor implications, but the job of Juvenile Justice is to serve children; we are not the Department of Labor. In other words, the Department of Juvenile Justice has the responsibility to make sure children are better served and provide the best methods to serve them, but not to make sure adults have employment. Unlike many of my associates, I believed we could accomplish both if we reformed the system.

That was my reality, but the truth was we needed more people fighting to keep kids out of trouble. That meant we needed staff to work differently. We did not need more adults telling kids in crisis to *Sit down, shut up, and do what I tell you to do.* We needed more trauma-informed, family-engaged people with a youth development framework who had the skills to communicate, do motivational interviewing, find and use opportunities to draw out information from the young people, then use the information gathered to create treatment plans that were solid and doable.

We needed to shift the entire system so young people who came into the system were there for a reason other than they mouthed off to an adult, usually a teacher, a police officer or a judge. There were many judges who considered Detention their personal "Time Out" corner a place to send disobedient, not delinquent, youth to teach them a lesson. I always thought it the most expensive lesson you can teach a young person, to take them from his or her family and lock the youth up to the tune of nearly $100,000 a year (even more in many states), sometimes with youth who had actually committed horrible acts. Some judges think kids need to experience the inside of a cell, that they need to know what it is to have those heavy doors lock behind them. I think that every judge should have to go through the degrading and often traumatic experience of being processed into a detention center and spend a night behind the locked doors before concluding that this is a fair and measured response to children exhibiting generally age appropriate adolescent behavior towards authority. Just a thought.

Current research from leaders in the field, Pew's Public Safety Performance Project, Annie E. Casey's Juvenile Detention Alternatives Initiative, and MacArthur's Models for Change has examined the historical and systemic roots of juvenile incarceration, especially for low level or non-offenders. No matter how you analyze the data, it is clear that every time a child passes the threshold of a secure facility, it raises the chances of returning for some greater offence and immediately reduces a child's opportunity to find success in education, career, and community. I was not willing to believe this was an "Acceptable" side effect of our work.

Fortunately for me, while I was trying to reimagine our Juvenile Justice system in anticipation of the renewed focus by the Task Force, I had the honor of being selected as a new fellow in the Annie E. Casey Foundation, Children and Family Fellowship program. This intensive and prestigious leadership program prepares innovative executives from sectors working to improve outcomes for children, families, and communities to use a results based leadership model to deliver better outcomes for the populations they serve. As a Fellow, I sharpened my own leadership skills with expert faculty and a dynamic group of peers who were leading change and reform efforts in education, child welfare, and justice systems. This experience reinforced my commitment to being a results-based leader and making Kentucky DJJ a results-based organization with the capacity to actually measure how much we were doing, how well we were doing it, and if any stakeholders (youth, families, communities) were better off because of our contribution. It seemed to be only way to actually assure the public that we were doing our best work.

Building on my idea about children leaving our system more whole, and not with more holes, I revealed a new results statement to my leadership team, *"All Kentucky children safe, supported, and provided a clear path to success."* Some were concerned that it was a broad statement that did not limit our work to just the walls and locked doors of Juvenile Justice. I was of the opinion that every agency and organization that had any responsibility for children and their wellbeing should have the same result in mind no matter if they worked the part of that population firmly on track in the cradle to career pipeline or if they were catching the children falling, jumping, or getting pushed into the school to prison pipeline. We should want the same outcome, our work should bring us to the same results, no matter what child we are looking at. That meant we needed more communication and sharing of resources between all our departments that serve children

A big issue was we still had youth coming to us for minor, often non-criminal infractions such as missing school, or a host of other typical teen behaviors. Kids with authority issues could easily trigger a justice response instead of a normal response to a teenager going through teenage issues. No matter how a youth arrived at the doors of DJJ, most young people stayed tied to our system until they were no longer able to return. It was often said that the best way to get off DJJ probation was to turn 18.

Although most of our staff wanted the opportunity to do better work and be of greater service to the youth we serve, there were still many employees only concerned about the possibility of losing their jobs or honestly believing we were being soft on crime. Some even made it clear that they were hired to punish bad children. They did not believe that kids being taken from their family and homes was punishment enough, and felt we needed to remind the imprisoned youth daily that they were monsters. It was this culture we were determined to reform, a culture that has crept into the fabric of America's Juvenile Justice systems over decades.

Fortunately, I knew there were some new promising partnership models starting implementation around the nation, collaborations that prevented youth from entering secure settings directly from schools or the courts in the case of non-criminal behavior. We were actively looking for a new way of addressing the problem and an opportunity to pilot an alternative.

Luckily, the court system in Henderson County, Kentucky decided that it wanted to be proactive in its work with and for the children in their jurisdiction. The chief judge contacted DJJ and requested our intervention and assistance after realizing their Courts was detaining youth who had committed status and other minor offenses at a rate that was much higher than other counties in the state.

A status offender is a young person who has made a bad choice, but if the young person were an adult, the same behavior would not be considered a crime. However, because the person making the bad choice is a child, the judge has the ability to sanction him or her. Typically the judge might order the youngster to comply with some conditions like go to school every day, don't curse your mom, or don't run away. If the youngster does not follow the orders, the judge could have him or her locked up. It is technically not the behavior itself that allows the child to be locked up, but the fact that once a judge tells you not to do something, and you do it, you're violating that judge's order. Violating a lawful court order allows a youth to be penalized as if the youth were criminal, including the option to have the child chained and transported to a secure detention facility by law enforcement personnel.

Many of these young people are dealing with problems at school or home and have experienced some level of trauma, drama, or pain in their lives. Too often they also have intellectual or developmental challenges or mental illnesses that have not been properly addressed or even diagnosed. Children who come into the system with these challenges can easily react with frustration, fear, and acting out. Those behaviors often elicit a physical response from staff, thus creating the likelihood of longer contact with the system.

Fortunately, armed with new skills to utilize Results Based Accountability, along with trained facilitators and faculty, I began to develop a strategic plan that would start us moving towards the change we wanted to see. The irrefutable and impartial Pew data showed us how our system components were colluding, subconsciously or unconsciously, to continue the criminalization of children. This meant our success rate, when measured in lives transformed, was very inconsistent.

I was determined things could be done differently. I sent a team from my staff to Henderson County to assist local officials in the courts and schools in their pursuit of improving their local system. Our DJJ team was committed to building a comprehensive system for Henderson County, which required them to conduct a hand count of all the courts juvenile files and create a computer system that would allow the court to track what they were doing with and for youth in a more meaningful way. Once the database was in place, it became clear which youth were being sent to detention and the reasons why.

The members of the Henderson County Support team demonstrated a true passion for the work they had accomplished. One was a member of my executive team and requested the opportunity to help Henderson County further by identifying or possibly creating potential programs that could be tested in Henderson County as a model for future partnerships. DJJ developed a pilot program utilizing our own resources. We reassigned one of our own community workers to the local high school as a support to students having problems. They were not School Resource Officers, but counselors or trained clinicians ready and willing to work for those kids who were academically challenged, removed from class for behavior problems, or who showed signs of trauma. We established a process within the school that allowed young people in crisis to receive a needs assessment and evaluation to determine if they should be referred out to a counselor or other support services.

The pilot was an immediate success and significantly lowered the number of young people coming out of the school system into the juvenile justice system. In the first year, the pilot saved the court system a significant amount of money and the school system enough real dollars that in order to ensure the work continued, the school district added a new position with district funding. It was a great demonstration of how systems partnering together could achieve results they could not individually. We began receiving requests from other districts to start replicating the program; we had hit upon a viable solution to reduce the number of young people coming from the schools into the judicial system.

Meanwhile, we kept exploring ways to bring positive change to other parts of the Juvenile Justice system. I had staff researching and brainstorming ways to bring some reform to our high security youth facilities. With the help of one of my most successful facility superintendents, we identified one young man we thought would make a good candidate for a new approach. The young man we selected had been with us since he was about 15. He had been charged as an adult with a crime that would keep him incarcerated until he was at least in his fifties. The truth is, without help, he would have never would have made it out of that system; we had a choice to make: Do we help him accept that truth or do we help him do the hard work of creating another option?

Finding a way to help him to become more whole meant that we were going to have to do things in a way we hadn't before. This young man was mentally sharp. He had finished his classes and earned his GED. We found ways to allow him to continue his education, including certifications in masonry and carpentry. To tend to his social and emotional development, we used pet therapy, and allowed him to have a pet for which he was the primary caregiver within the program. Through this relationship, we felt we could develop connection and empathy. We got him involved in a number of activities inside and outside the facility including community service projects to really allow him a real opportunity to give back to the community.

When he turned eighteen, we petitioned the court to allow us to keep him in the juvenile system until the age of twenty-one; there were some very rare precedents. We hoped this could be our new standard for youth who came to us charged as youthful offenders, meaning they were facing lengthy prison sentences after being convicted as an adult. Armed with new brain-based research and data from neuroscience, we now understood that up to the age of twenty-four or twenty-five, the brain is still developing. This is especially clear when it comes to the brain's decision-making capacity. We argued that given the changes we were seeing with this young man, if given a few more years, we'd be able to demonstrate even a more radical transformation. Our goal was to return this young man to society in a condition that allowed him to be a safe, positive, and an actively-producing member of society. The Court gave us that opportunity.

The first part of the process meant allowing this young man to have meaningful work outside of the facility one day a week. When that proved to be something he could handle, we went to two days until eventually he was spending most of his time outside of the facility working, learning, and growing in his capacity to manage his life without institutional interference. We hoped when he returned to stand before the court on his twenty-first birthday, he might have a realistic chance at exiting the system.

His original trial generated a great deal of emotion because of the harm he had committed. It was important we demonstrate to the judge that he was no longer the same person the justice system put on trial, that the system didn't always fail. He was an example of what could be accomplished when the system worked the way it ought to work.

Our job is to help young people find their way out of the system and to better themselves. DJJ should not be a holding pen for adult prison. While young people are in our care, if we do our job correctly, there exists an opportunity to rebuild and reclaim lives.

A Champion For Youth

It was clear to us all that our work was to reform the ways Kentucky treated youth accused of committing a crime. Soon we had a name for our work, Senate Bill 200. I had the pleasure to be interviewed on the KET show Connections by Renee Shaw and talked about this work:

"As we ramp up for Senate Bill 200, we have to consider services [that are] child-centered, trauma informed, family focused, and completely engaged in building the community once they leave us. Now we have the opportunity not just to hold them accountable, but actually hold them up, to create chances and opportunity for hope to live and thrive, and for them to believe that because they came to us, they can go on and still be something greater than they were when they came through the door."

When it came time for a vote on SB200, there were a number of folks who still did not want the bill to go through. There were some legislators who were trying to rally their bases to torpedo it. However, I had several opportunities to testify before the House and the Senate. For me, it became more and more clear that even though politically this was an extremely challenging bill to pass, and there were political reasons for a slower more measured way, the urgency spoke to us in the data. In 2014, the Kentucky Legislature voted to adopt SB200, and Gov. Steve Beshear signed it into law.

For me, the challenge of creating and passing SB200 and the reforming of the Kentucky juvenile justice system was done. I was proud of the work we had accomplished; it marked the beginning of a transformation in Kentucky's child-serving systems. But for me personally, it was the fulfillment of a dream and a commitment to contribute meaningfully to the juvenile justice state system before I went on to spread the word and create other great works. So I decided to resign my commission in April of 2014, leaving the implementation of this new vision to people in whom I was and am still confident will make all that we imagined a living part of this improved system.

What an honor to have led this agency to a place which punctuated my belief that young people with disabilities, trauma, and other challenges, along with young people who make non-lethal mistakes and bad and immature adolescent choices are not to be criminalized! Together, we've created real change, change which ensures that for every door locking these kids in, there will be another door that opens to let them out.

CHAPTER EIGHTEEN

A PASSION FOR PERFORMING

"The world is a complicated place, and there's a lot of division between people. The performing arts tend to unify people in a way nothing else does." David Rubenstein

Meanwhile Back on the Stage

People who know me as a professional in the child service field are often surprised when they learn that I have also maintained a strong performance portfolio since college. In fact, I have long used performing and speaking as a way to recharge and reenergize myself for the difficult fight that I have been waging in the justice system. One of the greatest benefits of my ADHD is that I have been able to juggle my family life, both national speaking and performance schedules, in addition to leading state and national advocacy and Juvenile Justice reform work. (While I was the Commissioner of Juvenile Justice, it was a little bit harder. I did limit my performing and speaking schedule significantly, but I used some of my vacation time to perform.)

I have had a passion for performing since the 7th grade when I was cast as the happy-go-lucky mailman in the Valentine's play. I only had one line as I made my cameo appearance and crossed the stage, *"I can feel it in my bones, it's going to be a Razzle Dazzle day!"* On that cue, I was to slip on a patch of imaginary ice, fly high into the air flinging and letting valentines rain down around me as I hit the floor. At the biggest performance, I hit my lines perfectly and flew into the air landing hard on the stage floor. The entire cafeteria was silent as I landed, then as the letters rained down upon me, the audience erupted into a roar of cheers, claps and screams. I remember laying there, taking in the glory and thinking, *"I like this!"*

Although I chose not to pursue theater as my profession, I decided years ago that it would continue to be my creative outlet. I was excited to discover a way to use my performance skills to balance my life. In law school, I realized that I could apply all of my acting skills in the courtroom, even once using a Shakespearian monologue for an opening. My theater training ensured the litigation and courtroom skills class was one place in law school my presence was not questioned. Like the boost Lorraine's Mental Math days at Horizons, using my talent for performing in Litigation Skills Class gave me confidence to weather the other challenges.

While I worked at Berea College after law school, I began developing my first one-man show, a Living History Chautauqua program with support from the Kentucky Humanities Council called *The Long Climb to Freedom*. Dreama and I researched, developed, and wrote this Chautauqua presentation based on the experiences and accomplishments of Angus Augustus Burleigh, chronicling his real life journey from his early childhood living free as the son of an English sea captain to his eventual capture and enslavement. Still a teenager during the Civil War, A. A. Burleigh escaped to the Union Lines, and enlisted in the military, thus ending his status as property. After the war, Berea's founder, John G. Fee invited Burleigh to Berea to participate in the Grand Experiment of building interracial kinship through shared living and educational opportunities.

On a personal level, I felt compelled to perform and share his story because A.A. Burleigh was Berea College's first African American graduate. Eventually the performance became the most popular and highly requested Chautauqua program on the KHC roster. Several other state Humanities Councils heard about my work, and soon I was performing *The Long Climb to Freedom* nationally.

It was not until I began to travel across Kentucky sharing the life of A.A. Burleigh that I realized how important these stories can be in the process of healing the often overwhelming division so many of our communities experience. Each audience created a completely new performance as I fed on the energy of the audience, whether it was apprehension, acknowledgement, sadness, or rage. I have shared the story of A.A. Burleigh more than five hundred times from college theater stages to living room rugs. There is a power to sharing our national story in this way, instead of the intellectual exercise that generally occurs when we sit down and attempt to "talk" about the stories of race and class in America.

Early in my career as a Chautauqua performer, I was invited to perform in a small town in western Kentucky. The program was to take place in an old converted church right on the Ohio River. I recounted the story of A. A. Burleigh's escape from slavery to join the Union forces at Camp Nelson, Kentucky and the many trials and tribulations he and others experienced to volunteer their lives to the Union cause with the hope of finding equality of voice and opportunity. As I took the stage, I noticed an elderly gentleman seated in the front row flanked on each side by his grandsons, he seemed visibly shaken. By the end of the performance, he was completely out of sorts.

As I greeted audience members, posing for pictures and signing program books, the old man, almost being carried by the towering boys on either side, struggled to straighten his bent frame to meet my gaze straight on. When he finally found the words to speak, I was completely unprepared for what happened next. As he reached for my hand, he began to sob uncontrollably, and I waited with him until he found the breath to speak. What he shared broke my heart and reaffirmed my faith at the same moment.

He began to tell the story of a fourteen-year-old boy who swept the floors at the train station each night, just a few hundred feet from the little church in which we stood in. On a cold winter night, a train came through late and discharged only one passenger - a black soldier dressed in his army uniform with a backpack full of gear. The little train station was the transfer point to switch from the north/south running train to catch one heading to the East coast port cities, where the soldier would most likely board a ship taking him across the Atlantic and into harm's way as the first World War began.

As the young boy continued to sweep the floor, the train manager approached and told him very directly, that under no circumstances was that nigger to step into the warm interior waiting area of the station. So the young boy stood and watched as an American soldier, on his way to lay his life on the line for the nation he believed in, stood outside in the freezing cold, treated like an outcast. The boy felt helpless to take the soldier the simplest comfort or thank him for his sacrifice.

As the old man finished the story, he could hardly breathe, and his grip on my arm had become vice-like. He looked at me and said, *"I've needed to tell that story for eighty years, and I want to know if you can forgive me for staying silent all this time, for not being brave enough to do something for that soldier who was preparing to sacrifice everything for my country and for my freedom."*

Modern day Chautauqua programs are historical presentations in which one is both scholar and actor. In every space I have performed, whether a small southern town square or the Yale Club in New York City, the response has been powerful. The opportunity to hear and understand unique experiences and perspectives unfiltered by intellectual justification creates a powerful conversation about a better America, the ideal we all strive for together.

After my performance in the persona of a historical person, I answer questions in character, sharing the deep level of research that is required to "become" a historical figure. Finally, I step out of character to answer questions about developing the research, the program, and additional details I could not share as the character. The Q&A usually ends with me telling a bit of my personal story and why I think it is important to share these incredible experiences with communities of lifelong learners.

Later on, as the Lexington Youth Violence Prevention Project, which was funded by a grant from the Knight Foundation, was coming to an end, it seemed like it was the perfect opportunity for me to return to performing both as a Chautauqua presenter and as a spoken word artist. I also wanted to explore new ways to use my art to engage, encourage, and empower youth by focusing their own creative voices. The Kentucky Arts Council honored me by selecting me as one of their teaching artists, and I began to work across the Southeastern United States with an arts and social justice organization called "Alternate ROOTS." As an artist in residence in schools and community centers, I provided youth and adults with opportunities to sharpen and share their theater storytelling and creative writing skills.

Reliving History

In 2001, there was growing attention to the Bicentennial of the Lewis and Clark Expedition, which would begin in 2003. In anticipation of the opportunity to be a part of this once in a lifetime experience, I began developing my second Chautauqua program *York, Explorer*. I partnered with the KHC again, and after an early performance for an audience that included members of the Lewis and Clark Bicentennial

Committee, I was invited to play a more significant role in the coming Commemoration. York was the only African American member of the Lewis and Clark expedition and thanks to a goldmine of newly discovered letters written by William Clark after the expedition, there was new information to share which would make York's story one of the biggest "New Voices" of the Bicentennial. For a video excerpt, go to http://0s4.com/r/JEI45M.

By 2003, the official beginning of the Bicentennial Commemoration, the National Parks Service had enlisted me as a regular presenter in their Tent of Many Voices, the performance venue of the nation's only mobile National Park called the Corps of Discovery II. We retraced the path of the expedition over the six-year arc from the Atlantic

(the Eastern Trail) to the Pacific and back into St. Louis. Throughout the Bicentennial, this was my home away from home and the rangers and engineers who operated the Corps of Discovery II became my second family. I portrayed York across the entire nation in small towns, Tribal communities, historic theaters, and most often on the stage under the Tent of Many Voices. The rangers told me that York was the most well attended

single program of the Bicentennial. They called it the "Hasan Davis" or the "York" protocol when they had to pack the performance tent chairs closer and bring in all their reserve seats. As for me, I just loved sharing York and instigating dialogue.

Along the trail, I was privileged to be welcomed in many of the Native communities the expedition visited two hundred years earlier. I listened and shared the stories of York's presence with elders and storytellers from many tribes. It was clear that his unique presence had a significant impact in many of these communities. I was "gifted" many times: Pendleton Blankets from the Umatilla, a Walking Stick from a representative of the Yankton Sioux, a hunting knife, a hand carved replica of a canoe, and a replica grizzly bear claw necklace. But the greatest honor I received was the privilege of carrying one of the Nation

Flags during the Parade of Native Nations at the National Bicentennial closing event. These are gifts and honors I will forever cherish.

No More Masks

As I shared the lives of Burleigh and York, I began to share parts of my own story too. As I became more aware of its potential power, and with continued encouragement from family and friends, I decided it was finally time for me to tell the story that I had been hiding from all but a few people for most of my life. I hoped that others who have experienced similar challenges might find strength and courage in my willingness to speak not just of the trials, but also of the many triumphs that I experienced.

I started speaking at churches, youth programs, schools, and summer camps, sharing my story with the young people and families they served. After Commissioner Ralph Kelly recommended me to the Governor for appointment to the Kentucky Juvenile Justice Advisory Committee, he arranged for me to be the keynote speaker at a national Juvenile Justice workers conference. (Go to http://0s4.com/r/HJ4R36 for a sample of one of my talks.) This opportunity to spend time with juvenile justice professionals from across the nation convinced me that there was plenty of good work to be done in the field. I also began to realize that my story really resonated with professionals in the child-serving profession as well. Mine was the example of the best and worst things that systems can do to children. State and national child-serving agencies and systems began inviting me to speak and participate in conferences and I began providing technical assistance to organizations wanting to improve their work with their youth and families.

As Chair of the Kentucky Juvenile Justice Advisory Board, formerly the Juvenile Justice Advisory Committee, and as an active member of the National Coalition for Juvenile Justice, I had the opportunity to increase my knowledge of the child-serving systems beyond my own experience of them. This allowed me craft my message of hope for those adults who everyday commit themselves to alleviating the Trauma, Drama, and Pain that is so prevalent in the lives of so many youth today.

The Final Piece of the Puzzle

In recent years, Colorado Humanities Council began to invite me to perform and give motivational talks across the state in its annual celebration of Black History Month. From the Front Range to the Western Slopes, I shared the stories of A.A. Burleigh and York as well as my own journey, especially with youth and young adults who were looking for more recent examples of triumph over tragedy. We provided programs for universities, community colleges, libraries, reentry programs, public schools, detention centers, theaters, and corporate offices. Over the three or four years, the stories have touched thousands of lives.

On one of my annual breaks from leading Kentucky's Department of Juvenile Justice, I returned to Colorado for another week of performances. We had a hectic 16 performances in 10 cities during a 7-day statewide tour with Denver as my home base. As I checked into the hotel, I noticed the colorful signs and posters of a conference put on by an organization called PEAK Parent Center, which provides support and training to individuals, families, and educators to ensure that all people with disabilities are fully included in their neighborhood schools, communities, employment, and all walks of life.

After walking around and reading the posters, I thought that this was my kind of group, but after meeting them, I was sure. After hanging out with them at their evening social event, they welcomed me into their group without hesitation or a registration, and invited me to sit in on some of the sessions. In-between my performance schedule, I spent time with this wonderful group of self-advocates, champions, and Hope Dealers. I left Colorado more inspired than ever, ready to get back to my "Real Job as Commissioner." A few months later, PEAK contacted me, saying they thought that I would be a perfect speaker for the 2015 nationally acclaimed Annual Conference on Inclusive Education.

It felt like coming home when I returned to the conference to give one of the keynotes. Finally, I had a stage to speak from where my experiences and story were not interpreted, but lived. The opportunity to recharge these champions and refuel these fierce self-advocates was a wonderful blessing for me. What was truly amazing was that I was welcomed and celebrated among people who didn't look sideways at my stories, but instead nodded furiously with understanding and empathy, or unapologetically laughed out loud before I told my embarrassing disability story because they already knew from their own experiences what went wrong maybe even worse. It was liberating and felt like the last tiny shard of my intricate mask was finally and permanently removed.

This is now my work. I perform and I speak, advise and consult. I tell stories that inspire, timeless stories of triumph over slavery and bigoted fear, and modern tales of hope in the face of overwhelming  despair. These are the stories that must be told! To watch a video of one of my talks, go to http://0s4.com/r/K1TZ5W.

CHAPTER NINETEEN

ON BEING A HOPE DEALER

A candle loses nothing by lighting another candle.

Father James Heller

Yet it multiplies the light and divides the darkness.

Hasan Davis J. D.

Don't Give Up!

I love traveling across this country to talk about Juvenile Justice and Education Reform. But as the crowds thin, I am often approached by youth champions so worn down you can see the look of being under siege in the slump of their shoulders. They ask, sometimes in soft whispers, like it's just between us, *"When is it okay to finally give up?"* I nod and sometimes offer a small touch, some way of acknowledging the obviously difficult and seemingly thankless mission of continuously pouring one's faith into a child like spring water into a leaking bucket. When I have the time, they talk while I listen to story after story of unsatisfying efforts to make a difference. Sometimes the efforts are derailed by the family in crisis, sometimes sabotaged by others who have already made up their mind what's to be done, and sometimes the child is so difficult that the sheer effort seems overwhelming. For another of my speaking presentations, go to http://0s4.com/r/LAFBQG.

It was in an effort to celebrate those beleaguered workers that I began to end my keynote or workshop with an invitation to stand up and join me on the floor for a celebration dance to honor all they have done, and to remind them that being a champion for these children is like wrestling an eight-hundred pound alligator. There are only two important rules to remember if you ever have the misfortune of facing off against an eight-hundred pound alligator.

• Rule #1: You don't give up when you get tired; you give up when the alligator gets tired.

• Rule #2: This alligator doesn't get tired! This work is difficult and rewarding, but it requires a massive dosage of hope. If it were easy, everyone would be willing to do it.

It is exciting to share stories of perseverance while speaking adamantly about the challenges young people face and the work adult champions must do to support youth in very meaningful ways. If we value the lives of youth entangled in the octopus-like systems of juvenile justice, public education, family welfare, behavioral, and mental health—all these systems must change. How do we stop marginalizing young people who have an experience with challenges like disabilities, poverty, or delinquency?

Today, it is customary for youth experiencing trauma to be treated as de-facto criminals, often sentenced to secure incarceration for their own protection or to "teach them a lesson." Systems once conceived as ways to harbor and heal our most vulnerable have become punitive systems causing irreparable harm to our most troubled children, their families, and our communities.

To Whom Much is Given

I am at a point in my journey where I can look back over the totality of my experiences from the kid locked in the coat room because of his disabilities, to getting expelled and removed from every educational environment I participated in, to a juvenile arrest, losing family to violence on the streets and now, to finally being a professional serving children in crisis.

I never imagined myself old, blessed with family, and the opportunity to enjoy their lives as they unfold so differently than mine. It amazes me to watch my sons experience the world and consume knowledge like I never could. Writing about my journey is one way to finally recognize all my Hope Dealers. I have named many of them in this

book, but I have so many more unsung, unnamed Hope Dealers, people who believed in spite of the facts that I could be more. Now, I want to pay it forward, be present and accountable, taking responsibility for providing another generation the opportunity to go even further.

When I was a teaching artist, I worked for over a month with the same group of young people. I led them through creative communication exercises and body improvisations, and then moved into more personal work like creative exploration. The process was designed to allow students to explore and acknowledge the challenges of their present experience while at the same time, imagining themselves actualizing their hopes, dreams, and better selves. I called this unanchored dream making. From there, we explored our aspirational futures through creative writing and goal setting. I later learned a new name for this process, "back casting," the practice of working step by step backwards from one's idealized self or desired outcomes to one's present circumstances. At each step, one must determine what skills, supports, and opportunities are required to reach the goal. When the group participants finally arrived at their present selves, they had developed a clear set of objectives, a road map if you will, to achieving their goals. This was only for the courageous.

I am reminded of a class I taught years ago and my conversation with a professional staffer who left me feeling sad and disappointed. I was upset by the conversation, but thankful she was willing to put her true thoughts out there so I could analyze my own feelings. One afternoon, just as the students were dismissed, the classroom teacher I was paired with commented, *"This has been such amazing work! I have never seen my students exploding with so much energy and passion about their futures. They are talking about themselves in ways I never would have imagined possible. But do you think it's fair?"*

"What do you mean?"

"You know - to give them all that false hope?"

"Huh?" was all I could push out.

"Well, they're talking about all the amazing things they are going to be and the impact they want to have on the world. But, just between you and me," she leaned in and lowered her voice to a whisper as if the next words were a secret everyone knew, but were forbidden to speak of. *"You know that's not in the cards for them, right? Do you think it's fair to keep feeding them and getting them so excited about who they could be every day, and then send them back out into a world that's not going to let them become any of those things?"*

Her matter of fact revelation almost shattered me. Sean's voice echoed through my head. In that moment, I panicked, trying to imagine how many others wading into the battle for our children each day never believed they could actually win. Were these individuals only hoping to provide some temporary respite for these desperate and doomed children, believing just enough so they can comfort themselves for at least making their poor lives a little better before returning them to their broken realities?

I recently thought about a friend who has worked many years as a hospice care worker. When I learned about the principles of her work, it sounded a lot like the words so many child-serving professionals espouse. Both attempt to provide the "damned, doomed, and dying" a meaningful end of life experience. Too many adults with power and influence over the success of children have accepted the idea that their best work is actually hospice, not hope.

When that teacher challenged my work as an exercise in false hope, I was beside myself, first angry, then concerned. I had to unpack the statement myself before I could emphatically reject her notion as wrong-minded. I went home and began my search. First, I checked out Merriam Webster for a definition of false. False *adjective*: 1. not real or genuine; 2. not true or accurate; deliberately untrue: done or said to fool or deceive someone; 3. based on mistaken ideas. Then, I looked up the word hope. Hope *verb*: to want something to happen or be true and think that it could happen or be true.

I reflected on my philosophy class at Berea and the section on analysis of faulty logic. It struck me that there was some faulty logic at work here and it seems to have been ignored for a long time. I was trained in law school to break down and rebuild statements in order to construct a plausible, even stronger counterargument. This is how I approached the false hope phenomenon.

So, if hope is defined as belief in future possibilities, believing one can make that future happen. It is a future lying statement, a statement that cannot be false, only present or absent. If it is present, it is called hope. If it is absent, it is not false hope; that is hopelessness.

My conclusion: There is no such thing as false hope, not if we stay committed to our presence as Hope Dealers. The alternative to hope is hopelessness, and it has become a too common an experience for our youth. So many people who work with challenging children make hopelessness their mantra. Hopelessness creates a seething void and allows chaos to continue unchecked in their lives. Hope cannot be false, just unrealized, waiting on the edge of our interactions ready to take root.

Encouraged and renewed with an even deeper clarity of purpose, I returned to work with my students and give teachers the example of hope in what they often see as a hopeless situation. So although the teacher's attitude first had me panicking, I was grateful for the opportunity to reevaluate the goal of the work we do with and on behalf of students.

To those who work with our children and our teenagers, there may come a time in your career when you feel you no longer have the ability to believe without proof, or shine light into darkness. Maybe, like my vocational rehabilitation counselor at law school, you feel guilty for not reigning in some poor soul who was dreaming beyond personal capability because you fear the person might backslide or fail again, and someone in charge might blame you.

Ultimately, hope is a thing we choose to give willingly. We must give and spread it widely. Hope cannot be false, not if you truly deeply believe. Only then will you be able to speak light into every dark corner you see, to believe deep inside that it could ignite a fire of possibility because you could be that right person who puts it to a struggling youth just the right way, like my mom and Lorraine did for me. If you keep it simple and keep repeating the message of believing, of hope, eventually it gets heard and that child who is feeling defeated discovers a reason to work towards that future and the next best thing.

Hope is a central theme of my story. It helped me overcome many obstacles. My mother was there carrying hope for me until I was brave enough to carry it for myself and for others. She encouraged me to decide if I carried enough hope to walk bravely towards the unknown, or if I was so fearful of my differentness that I would huddle in the dark and continue to lash out at a cruel world. She could not guarantee my acceptance. All she could do was ensure there were more images of me to compare myself to than the few I had been offered so many times by others as a child. She provided an image that was bright and beautiful to light my path.

Like my mother, you will not be able to guarantee your belief and passion will change a child's life. However, having weighed in on a child's side, you have to let him or her walk, run, and then fly. Then fall. Then walk. Then run. We have to let children do this, knowing that if all things being equal, and we put enough energy into them, if it's going to happen, it's going to happen great. It gives us the courage to find the next child, or the next person who needs that support, and not hold back because of that one time it didn't work. Be willing to go all in again. I think that is the real gift of what we do. *Inevitable Victory.*

A few years ago, I came across that bandana my mother sent me at Berea. It was thrown into a box affectionately labeled "College Stuff." I was excited to see it because I feared it was lost in the ten or so moves I made since becoming an adult. I immediately vacuumed sealed it in a plastic freezer bag to keep those precious words from completely fading away. I now have that bandana framed and hanging on my wall to be reminded of the many ways hope can manifest to the lost and the seeking. *Inevitable Victory for Hasan. With Love, Mom.*

EPILOGUE

WHERE ARE THEY NOW?

"Believe and act as if it were impossible to fail."

Charles F. Kettering

Update 2015: A Deeply Blessed Family

My mother, Alice Lovelace, is the epitome of what I aspire to be as a Hope Dealer, creating doors of possibility where others could only imagine locks. In the years since she began working as writer-in-residence at The Neighborhood Arts Center, she has helped to create or lead local, national, and international organizations devoted to arts, education, and social justice. She has a mantel full of awards and recognition for her work as a poet, arts administrator, and organizer. In 2000, I attended her graduation and watched  as she was awarded a Master's degree from Antioch University in Yellow Springs, Ohio. Even though she says she is retired, she continues to serve as Chairperson of the Board for the Southeast Community Cultural Center that she helped found thirty-one years ago. She also continues her work as a co-editor at *In Motion Magazine*, an on-line journal devoted to issues of democracy (www.inmotionmagazine.com).

My baby sister Shawnta earned her Accounting Degree at Berea College. In Kentucky, she worked at Forward in the Fifth, a nonprofit that unites people and communities to create positive change. When she married, she moved to Covington, Georgia and works with children with disabilities in Newton County as a special education paraprofessional, under the guidance of a special education teacher. She is in the final semester of her work on a Master's Degree in Special Education.

Tony, my youngest brother, like me, found high school to be a challenge. Despite this, he developed his intuitive sense of color and décor to become a popular interior designer in Atlanta. He also creates electronic dance music, works as a DJ, and a few years ago, wrote the music score for one of the Spiderman video games.

Theresa, the oldest of our biological siblings, taught at Horizons School for over twenty years. She reclaimed her love for poetry thirteen years ago after the loss of our father, Charles "Jikki" Riley. Since his death, she has emerged as a nationally recognized slam poet, youth advocate, and teacher of poetry. Theresa co-founded the Art Amok Slam Team, and has competed in multiple national and regional competitions, culminating in 2011, when she took first place in the *Women of the World Poetry Slam Competition.* She was named the 2012 *McEver Chair in Poetry* at Georgia Tech University. In May 2013, Sibling Rivalry Press published her first full collection of poems. *After This We Go Dark* became an American Library Association Honoree, and the book can now be checked out in local and college libraries around the world.

Dreama and I have been building our important work together over the last quarter century. Dreama has become my rock, one of the reasons I am able to find success in my chosen work; she deftly picked up where all of my other champions left off. She has helped me rebuild the

world on my own terms, partnering with me in marriage and in work in the belief that I could achieve my greatest expectations. Dreama is a tremendous success, herself, in her work with and for children and families in the region and across the country. As a national leader in rural education, an architect of models for educating youth in widespread rural environment with high poverty, she accepts none of the traditional excuses or folksy anecdotes. Each day, education leaders across the nation see her creating successful models of schools and communities where some thought it impossible. She is, without question, a rock star in her field, a Hope Dealer with an exponential multiplier effect. It is a blessing to be on a mission together, to be partners working toward the same outcomes for our youth across the state, the region, and the nation as the outcomes we expect for our own two sons.

When they were in their teens, *Derrick and Sean* joined the Atlanta Chapter of the Guardian Angels, a citizen vigilante group that formed in New York City. They both rose to positions of authority in the organization. I was excited to see them doing great things. They were protecting their community from pimps, pushers, and predators. I knew then and continue to believe there is compassion and greatness in my brothers, but there was more fear of trying and failing.

Today, *Derrick* has found his path to leadership inside prison helping younger inmates to find a safe way to navigate the system toward reentering society prepared to stay as productive citizens. He has completed multiple education courses working towards a bachelor's degree. He has been in a number of programs and clubs including the Gavel Club, an offshoot of the International Toastmasters professional speakers program. He is currently in an experimental program for model prisoners, which has the potential to allow him an early release. I recently had the opportunity to reunite him with his son, Derrick Junior, and his daughter, Amber. Both are doing well and making their own ways in the world.

My brother Sean has finally received the treatment and support that he deserved. He has embraced his innate intelligence and developed the writing and thinking skills he never allowed himself time to develop before prison. He has written two novels, and is studying philosophy, history and meditation.

On the Next Horizon

I believe deeply in the possibility of tomorrow. I don't want to just focus on what's present right now because that's just a test for the moment. When we look forward, there is always possibility. That is what we have to hold onto. We have to have hope in a better tomorrow, and have faith in our abilities and the abilities of those around us. That is what Lorraine was saying. That is what my mama held onto. My mother has been a Hope Dealer for many people in her life. Her focus on future possibilities allowed her biological children to survive and flourish, and she tried her very best with Sean and Derrick. Had she had more time, had she had them under her wing earlier, I don't doubt they too would have found their paths.

I too am a Hope Dealer, contributing to the growth of young people across this nation and the professional development of those who influence them. I provide that message in conference keynotes and workshops in places as diverse as state conferences on juvenile justice, colleges, houses of worship, museums, and school districts across the nation. I tell everyone I meet that every child in America deserves to be engaged, empowered, and provided a clear path to his or her greatest personal success in education, career, and community life.

When I finally visited my brother Sean in prison, we had a lively conversation in the visitation yard. Just like when I visit Derrick, I sat across from him and closed my eyes as he talked. As I pressed my mental "Reset" button, I heard his voice grow stronger as he talked us back into childhood. His tired battered body began to fill with a youthful vigor, his grey beard darkened, and those sad hopeless eyes narrowed with purpose. In that moment, not even a twenty foot wrapped in razor wire could contain us, because for a few moments, we are back in our childhoods, moving through the world as if there is one mind between us.

I was in the middle of this remembering when Sean suddenly started laughing (cackling actually) uncontrollably. He was retelling the story about that night in the pickup truck, about the time I would not just let him smoke those clowns who were disrespecting us, because I always tried to talk my way out of stuff instead of just dealing with the problem. During his highly animated reenactment of the scene, he was laughing so hard I wasn't sure if he could still breathe. All at once, he became disturbingly serious. Turning to me, he asked, *"Do you know what I wish?"* Completely surprised by his quick and dramatic change in demeanor, I just waited. *"I wish that I could have believed Mama when she told me that I was great."* I was speechless. *"I wish I had known how much she actually believed it when she said it."*

Every day in America, thousands of our children are drained from the robust cradle to career pipeline and flushed down some other pipeline of criminal justice, poverty, race, or disability. We can do better. For our children, our families, and our communities, it is time for us to say there are no more acceptable losses, no more children written off.

AFTERWORD

TOP TIPS

FROM SPECIAL EDUCATION ADVOCATE

AND PUBLISHER

YAEL COHEN, MA

AUTHOR OF #1 BESTSELLING BOOK

Secrets of a Special Education Advocate: Supercharge Your Child's Special Ed IEP So Your Child Can Excel

Hasan Davis first told me his story last winter as I interviewed him for a podcast for parents of kids with disabilities; the book grew from there. I didn't know much about him before we began to talk, but was fascinated with his story. Over the months watching his book come to life, I have been stunned, impressed, appalled, and fascinated over and over again. I'd like to share some of my thoughts with you and some important tips if you are an Advocate or Hope Dealer for a school-age child with learning challenges.

Hasan started school before the first special education law in the US in 1976, a law that six million kids in this country benefit from at any given moment. Certainly many of our schools today are much better for many children, but for others, we've still got a long way to go. Sadly, there are still children put into coatrooms and closets, or locked away in segregated classrooms. There are still children and youth who sit in classes year after year, waiting for an education, waiting for a specialized program that teaches kids to read, and encountering not enough trained staff. In most states, that school to prison pipeline for kids at risk still exists. Luckily for thousands and thousands of children, Hasan Davis has made it his mission to set a humane and useful juvenile justice system in place across the United States. Through his consulting and his dramatic conference keynotes, and now writing, I can't imagine he won't accomplish it!

Almost forty years after the first special education law was passed, special education is still not fully funded, and schools do not have the resources they need. With strict school reform and zero tolerance movements, there are still many children who simply are left behind. Many of these children do not have strong advocates, like Hasan's mother, Alice Lovelace, who kept pushing his schools to educate him. Even as schools hand parents a copy of their "rights," they may be encouraged to break those rights with secret meetings and weak educational goals.

As I read about Hasan's mother, Alice, pushing back to keep Hasan out of a special education class, I thought about a first grader who I recently helped parents keep out of a segregated classroom and to keep in her neighborhood school where she has friends and made great growth last year. The staff said they didn't know how to teach her, and thought the answer might a class in another school. Instead, she will remain with her friends, her hours of specialized instruction jumped from twenty minutes a day to 2 hours day, and everyone from the paraeducator to the teachers and the therapists will receive training. Some of the school staff has expressed excitement about the new skills they will have. As for the child, she deserves an education.

As I read about an instructor unfairly targeting Hasan for plagiarism, I thought about a high school student who currently is one of a growing list of kids with disabilities targeted by a local teacher who is allowed by her principal to threaten an otherwise "A" student with failing the course — for ostensibly "plagiarizing" one sentence out of hundreds.

I kept wondering, as I read, since we know how to teach kids with dyslexia how to read now; why do we have so many kids in our schools who can't read or spell and they don't receive the methodologies they require to learn?

I've also thought about race, other biases, and white-privilege. If we're not the ones affected by these, we can spend a lifetime not even noticing they exist.

Most of all, I've thought about resilience. Here was a little boy with so many strikes against him to succeed in school and in life, but with the help and support of a strong mom and other strong "Hope Dealers," Hasan not only beat the odds, but he succeeded in saving so many other children from our systems — and they are all OUR children. How many other children do we still miss, children who are written off? Can we take the chance of missing even one?

After performing almost thirty years of special education advocacy, after studying in those same university BA and MA programs that produce some of the very same people who tell you "No" at special education IEP meetings, and after hearing more crying and feisty moms on the phone than you can imagine from all over the country, I've developed the key top eleven tips I have learned which help parents advocate more effectively for their own children:

1) When at all possible, if you at all can, it pays to resolve differences with the schools without resorting to the legal system. Just because there are laws about special education doesn't mean that you'll win in a due process and that much will change. There are often other options. Sometimes you

have no choice and good legal decisions can make a difference for kids across the country (while a bad decision can hurt as many).

2) Don't believe everything the testing tells you about your child. There are dozens of reasons why a child might test a certain way. Your child is not a number. Also, know that schools often don't do all the testing a private provider would and they also may not tell you everything the testing indicates. That's why it is so important to get outside help to make sure you understand.

3) Never ever go to a special education meeting by yourself, especially because you will almost always be outnumbered. Take an advocate, a friend, or a relative who can ask questions and take notes. Be aware that a knowledgeable advocate can get you things you didn't even know existed; it's because we often go to a variety of meetings in a variety of districts.

4) Don't believe it's not about the money. Of course it's about the money; special education costs a lot of money. Your child still deserves an education.

5) Don't use the word "best" — your child is not entitled to the "best" education, only what's appropriate, so use "appropriate." (Otherwise the school may literally start talking about a Chevy and a Cadillac, which gets the conversation off track.) Bite your tongue if the school starts saying they want the best for your child; they're allowed to use the word.

6) A "no" from a special ed teacher or administrator means "Go up to the next level." They may be able to help. Don't just give up.

7) If it's not in writing, it didn't happen. This goes for what the school or district promises you, and also for evaluations. If you put that request in writing, the 60-day clock to complete it starts ticking. (I also now audio-record all the special education meetings I go to; it makes remembering what we said easier in case of disagreement later. I hardly ever listen to them again, but when needed, they are invaluable. It's not to threaten; it's simply a record and let the school know you'll be recording ahead of time.)

8) Be sure to get a copy of any information the school is going to use in your upcoming, including a draft IEP if the school is going to use one. Plot out the progress your child has, especially if the same test is used

more than once. If you don't have good information, you cannot fully participate in the meeting and in decision-making for your child.

9) Keep an organized copy of everything you get; it helps you track, and if you ever hire an advocate, a consultant, or an attorney, it makes conveying information much easier.

10) Behavior is the biggest issue in schools. Do not allow the school to play a "blame game." Stay focused on problem solving. Ask for a functional behavior assessment and all the data, not just the summary; you'd be surprised what you can learn.

11) No matter how angry you get, do not threaten due process at a meeting (unless you have already discussed your case with a special education attorney and you have a case). Disagreeing doesn't necessarily mean it's necessarily against the law.

And most important, remember to be your child's Hope Dealer!

For more information, go to www.gcticptips.com for a free video series for parents of kids with special needs and/or learning challenges.

PHOTOS

91560707R00111

Made in the USA
San Bernardino, CA
30 October 2018